Nursing guide to veterinary intensive care

Daniel Holden
BVetMed DVA DipECVA CertSAM MRCVS

Henston

Henston

Produced in association with *Hill's Pet Nutrition, Ltd

Henston
A Division of Veterinary Business Development
Olympus House
Werrington Centre
Peterborough
PE4 6NA

Telephone: +44 (0) 1733 325522
Facsimile: +44 (0) 1733 325512
e-mail: henston@vetsonline.com

Designed and produced by Veterinary Business Development Ltd

ISBN 1 85054 197 3

Price £7.50

Acknowledgements

All photographs are reproduced with permission from Hill's Pet Nutrition, Ltd. except where otherwise credited.

About the author

Daniel Holden BVetMed DVA DipECVA CertSAM MRCVS

Dan qualified from the Royal Veterinary College (RVC) in 1991. After a year in mixed practice, he returned to the RVC for a year as an intern and then completed a year's residency in clinical pharmacology. After a further period in practice, Dan undertook a residency in anaesthesia and critical care at Bristol, gaining the RCVS Diploma in Veterinary Anaesthesia in 1997. He then spent four years as a lecturer in small animal emergency medicine and intensive care at Bristol, where his duties included primary care of small animal emergencies, and management of the small animal intensive care unit. Dan gained the RCVS Certificate in Small Animal Medicine in 2001 and became a Diplomate of the European College of Veterinary Anaesthesia in 2002. He now divides his time between teaching for a veterinary continuing education company, and emergency and critical care medicine in private practice. He is a contributor to the BSAVA Manual of Small Animal Anaesthesia and Analgesia, *and* Manual of Small Animal Emergency and Critical Care, *and is one of the founding members of the European Veterinary Emergency and Critical Care Society.*

Contents

Foreword

That you are holding in your hands this practical guide, means that you are witness to two important developments in veterinary medicine in recent years. First is the growing recognition of support staff and the invaluable part they play. Secondly, it is clear that intensive and emergency care are no longer the monopoly of dedicated university units, but are increasingly found in private practice. This is positive progress.

Dan Holden is an expert in critical care; he is at the forefront of advancing knowledge of this important sector. In this book, he guides readers through the central aspects of intensive and emergency care, from setting up a specialist unit to an incident of cardiac arrest, with sensible and straightforward advice. Recommendations are designed to be transferred straight into practice; the clinical sections highlight the necessary precautions and actions in saving the lives of critically ill animals. This book will provide, again and again, the basis for making the right decisions in situations where time is short. Above all, it will help to prepare the environment necessary for dedicated staff to give effective and efficient care and support to animals.

Thanks go to Penelope Lyons, David Weaver and Mike Fleming for their valuable contributions to the successful production of this publication.

Peter Mueller MBS VetMed MRCVS

1 General principles of intensive care

Intensive care can be defined as 'a service for patients with potentially reversible conditions who can benefit from more detailed observation and intensive or invasive treatment than can safely be provided with general hospitalisation.'

There is no doubt that intensive care can be both labour-intensive and expensive. However, significant results can be achieved by aggressive primary management, attention to detail, good communication and often without sophisticated monitoring equipment. The last few years have seen an increased public desire (and demand) for higher levels of treatment; more pets are insured and standards of veterinary care are dramatically improving with the advent of increased continuing education. Media attention to human intensive care and veterinary care in general has also increased public awareness to an unprecedented level.

Establishing an intensive care facility

Setting up an intensive care unit (ICU) involves several considerations, each of which is discussed under a separate heading below.

Location within the practice

There may be no choice, but ideally ICU facilities should be adjacent to surgical and radiographic areas, and should not be part of a thoroughfare (Figure 1). This latter consideration limits traffic. Accessibility from other areas of the practice is important, but no direct external access should be present.

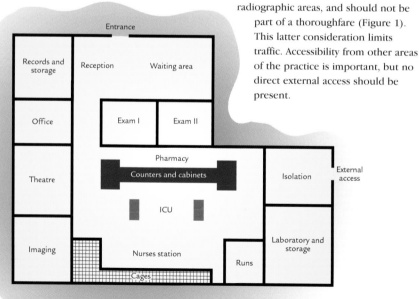

Figure 1 Location of an ICU in a clinic

Size

This ultimately depends on space and caseload. Facilities may be restricted to one or two kennels or beds, or a whole room may be available for use. Approximately 15% of all hospitalised patients are likely to require intensive therapy and management; unit size should therefore ideally represent 15% of total ward or kennel space.

Layout

Ideally, there should be a central treatment area and central nurses station; this allows more constant monitoring and permits full visibility of all cage areas. Storage space is located under treatment tables and around the periphery of the room.

Cages arranged in a single bank makes viewing easier. Wide, shallow cages make patients more visible and, ideally, smaller patients should not be caged above eye level. Separate mobile cots that can be moved around the unit are valuable for high-input, more unstable patients. Although walk-in cages are sometimes difficult to nurse in, they are the most suitable option for larger patients. Underfloor heating may be useful in these cages.

A minimum of two power points per cage is usually acceptable. Overhead blocks mounted centrally above the treatment areas are useful and prevent tangled cabling. Waterproof sockets (such as those designed for outdoor use) are expensive but very effective in areas likely to get wet. Socket blocks can also be mounted on patient monitors if necessary. Some form of auxiliary power may also be an option, depending on the budget.

If high-input patients requiring ventilatory support are anticipated, wall or ceiling-mounted piped gases save floor-space and make the administration of oxygen easier at multiple points around the unit. Piped medical air, oxygen and wall-mounted suction are ideal. If any procedures involving volatile agents (including nitrous oxide) are to be preformed in the unit, active waste gas scavenging is mandatory.

Unit structure and layout can have a significant effect on hygiene. Adequate drainage from cages should be ensured, and all surfaces should be easily cleanable. Avoid tiled floors as cracks will occur and thorough cleaning is more difficult. A static strip across the floor at the unit entrance reduces contamination from footwear and trolleys. Facilities for dehumidification and air-conditioning also tend to reduce the environmental bacterial load (if properly maintained).

Staffing requirements

As the speciality of intensive care grows in depth and sophistication and public awareness of available treatments for pets increases, it is clear that some form of intensive care focus is likely to become central to all large first and second-opinion veterinary facilities. Specialists in other fields (notably surgical specialists) are also beginning to appreciate the benefits of having suitably trained clinicians and nursing staff to reduce the demands on their professional time and provide appropriate care for high-input patients.

It is extremely difficult to over-emphasise the importance of well-trained, compassionate and efficient nursing staff in running a good intensive care unit. Nurses are, without doubt, the most vital members of an ICU team, as they have primary responsibility for patient care. Nurses are also best placed to rapidly detect adverse trends in patient status and need to be technically skilled as well as compassionate and efficient.

Working as a nurse in a veterinary intensive care unit is potentially stressful and challenging; it necessitates antisocial and often long hours and frequent contact with distressed, emotional and often highly demanding clients. Adequate experience and training (in clinical and non-clinical aspects) are essential. Good intensive care depends on a low patient : nurse ratio, which can be tiring, as 24-hour nursing cover is necessary for effective ICU function. Every effort should be made to avoid ridiculous working hours; shift-based systems are essential rather than an 'on-call' system. Shift start and end times should overlap to ensure all relevant clinical information is transferred.

What constitutes an ICU case?

Patients requiring intensive care and therapy often fall into one of three categories of animal.

1   Patients with moderate to severe pre-existing complications (e.g. cardiac, hepatic or renal disease) undergoing routine investigations or surgery: these animals require a greater degree and frequency of monitoring in the perioperative period than fit, healthy patients, because their reduced physiologic reserve means that complications are more likely to occur. Such patients at risk of developing complications may be admitted for observation – simple and frequent monitoring facilitates rapid intervention and reduces mortality. These patients are often post-surgical and are usually short-term ICU cases.

2   Stable patients needing extensive nursing care (e.g. wound care): these animals may require regular dressing changes or other checks requiring restraint or sedation. These individuals will be long-stay patients due to the nature of their injury or illness and are, therefore, at an increased risk of developing nosocomial (hospital-acquired) diseases. Patients needing complex and frequent nursing care are justifiable admissions; these cases are often managed better in a well-organised ICU due to the readiness and central location of materials and equipment. Such patients are often long-term ICU cases and are often prone to complications (sepsis, poor nutrition), which are most easily be managed in an ICU environment.

3   Severely unstable patients are obvious ICU candidates (major trauma, cardiorespiratory dysfunction, renal dysfunction, sepsis) and conform to the recognised ICU image of crisis management and potentially rapid response. These patients require constant and possibly invasive monitoring, possible respiratory support, fluid therapy, frequent blood and urine samples, aggressive infection control, analgesia, nutritional support and a high level of nursing input. In the human intensive care environment, a patient : nurse ratio of 1 : 1 or 2 : 1 usually exists.

Assessment of the emergency or critically ill patient

When one or more acutely ill or injured patients present as an emergency, it is possible for the situation to descend into chaos. Triage is a system that permits selection of patients according to the severity of their illness or injury, and allows them to be prioritised in order of urgency.

The essential aim is not to attempt a definitive diagnosis but to manage the life-threatening problems first. This ordered approach improves the level of primary care, avoids missed diagnoses, and saves money through shorter patient stays.

Preparation for the emergency

It is essential to have a dedicated space or area where new arrivals or acutely deteriorating patients can be resuscitated. This area should be adequately equipped and the following items are strongly recommended:

- oxygen and a means of delivery (also allows positive pressure ventilation)
- endotracheal tubes and stylets for difficult intubations
- intravenous fluids, emergency drugs and equipment for gaining intravenous access
- suction in some form
- chest drainage equipment
- cut-down pack or similar small surgical pack
- facilities for warming or cooling patients as necessary
- sample pots for blood, urine, faeces and fluid.

Questions to ask

A great deal of useful information can be obtained (usually over the telephone) before the animal arrives by asking simple questions. This can allow more specific preparation so that the emergency can be more effectively managed on arrival. For animals already hospitalised, relevant information should be easily extracted from the patient's notes.

Pertinent questions include:

- What are the breed, age, sex of the animal?
- Is he/she conscious or responsive?
- Is he/she breathing?
- Is he/she bleeding from anywhere?
- Is he/she currently taking any medication?
- Is he/she vomiting or retching?
- When did he/she last eat or drink?
- When did he/she last urinate?

Advice to give

Useful advice can be given to help minimise any further injury or deterioration in the animal's condition:

- muzzle if possible and necessary
- transport recumbent trauma patients on a flat rigid surface to minimise further displacement of any spinal column injuries

- apply pressure to obvious bleeding points
- cover open wounds, fractures or exposed organs with clean cloth
- bring packaging of suspected toxins with the patient
- keep the animal well padded during transport.

On arrival

Take the animal to the emergency or consulting room. If multiple cases arrive simultaneously, they should be seen in order of urgency, not in order of arrival (this concept is the basis of triage). Patients that are or appear to be dead on arrival at the clinic should receive priority, if only to confirm their demise and counsel the owner. The following is a list of presenting syndromes that require urgent attention:

- respiratory distress
- neurological abnormalities (seizures, coma)
- severe vomiting
- very fast or very slow heart rate
- bleeding from body orifices
- pale mucous membranes
- progressive abdominal enlargement
- severe coughing
- extreme pain
- inability to urinate.

A pertinent history should be obtained by reception or nursing staff from the owner, expanding on previous information gained from the initial telephone contact. Written consent should also be obtained for:

- any treatment (including surgery)
- resuscitation (closed and open-chest if appropriate)
- euthanasia if and when appropriate.

This may entail further discussion with the owner once an initial assessment of the patient has been made.

Patient assessment

The following pattern of prioritised assessment can and should be applied to any acutely deteriorating patient; it is equally applicable to hospitalised patients receiving treatment, and emergency patients at first presentation.

Patient assessment consists of:

- primary survey
- secondary survey
- definitive physical examination
- appropriate tests.

Primary survey

This should always follow the established pattern and address three fundamental questions.

Primary survey

Airway – Does the patient have a patent airway?

Breathing – Is the patient making regular coordinated efforts to breathe?

Circulation – Does the patient have a palpable or audible heartbeat and palpable pulses?

If the answer to any of these questions is 'no', the patient has impending or established respiratory or cardiorespiratory arrest and a full cardiopulmonary–cerebral resuscitation protocol should be adopted unless or until the owner dictates otherwise.

Secondary survey

This involves evaluation of the major body systems:

- respiratory
- cardiovascular
- central nervous system.

Respiratory assessment

Airway

The animal's airway should be considered to extend from the nose to the end of the trachea. Presentation of airway-related respiratory distress may vary according to cause and the animal's level of consciousness, but generally problems fall into two classes: obstruction (generally much more common) and disruption.

Obstructive causes include:

- foreign body (blood clot, vomit, saliva)
- mass (neoplasia, haematoma, abscess)
- trauma
- oedema or paralysis.

Disruption or rupture of the airway can occur with penetrating wounds or bites, and also with blunt thoracic trauma resulting in stretching and avulsion of the airways. The thoracic inlet and tracheal bifurcation are common sites for tears; punctures in the cervical region also occur. Major airway damage within the thorax often results in rapid death, but some patients may survive until presentation.

Rapid management of airway disorders is essential. Suction can often be invaluable and oxygen therapy often calms patients (especially cats). Trans-tracheal oxygen can be administered below the level of obstruction if the upper airway is affected; the following items should be assembled and kept within reach to allow rapid access to the tracheal lumen and rapid connecting to an anaesthetic breathing system:

- 14G needle + 2 ml syringe barrel + 7 mm Portex endotracheal tube connector.

Equipment to perform endotracheal intubation should be readily available at all times. This should include flexible guidewires and a wide range of tube sizes.

Breathing

Dogs and cats with respiratory distress are often anxious and prone to sudden deterioration. Cats, in particular, may be fractious and even the most minor procedures may result in a respiratory crisis. Careful management is, therefore, essential if complications are to be avoided.

Investigative approach

As with many varieties of emergency, a definitive diagnosis is not always essential and it is more important to localise the problem to the affected area of the respiratory tract (upper airways, small airways, pleural space, chest wall, pulmonary parenchyma). In most cases, this can be achieved by careful observation and thorough physical examination.

Observation

A normal cat or dog should have a respiratory rate of 15–30 breaths per minute with little chest wall movement. Clinical signs of respiratory distress can include:

- tachypnoea (very rapid breathing, often the only sign in cats)
- panting or mouth breathing
- discoloured mucous membranes
- stridor (noisy inspiration due to narrowing of the upper airway) or stertor (snoring-type noises due to obstructions)
- anxiety, aggression or restlessness
- paradoxical abdominal movement (abdominal wall moves inwards during inspiration)
- orthopnoea (standing with extended head and neck, abducted elbows) in dogs.

Examination

Examination should be thorough but as stress-free as possible. Careful palpation of the external nasal cavity, pharynx, larynx and neck should be performed and chest wall movement with respiration should be noted. Mucous membranes and capillary refill should also be assessed.

Auscultation is an art form and potentially invaluable; nursing staff should practice as often as possible and learn to recognise abnormal sounds. Auscultate the whole airway from the nasal passages to the lungs, and wet the hair to improve contact of the chestpiece. Be prepared to return the patient to an oxygen source quickly (if necessary) for rest and recovery.

Abnormal lung sounds

Crackles – usually inspiratory and due to re-opening of small airways during expiration. Crackles may be fine or loud and coarse.

Wheezes – fine, often high-pitched inspiratory or expiratory sounds produced by bronchial and bronchiolar narrowing.

Rhonchi – lower pitched inspiratory or expiratory sounds produced by air movement through larger airways. Normal after exercise or if the patient is excited.

Careful auscultation of the heart is essential to rule out a cardiac cause for the dyspnoea (difficulty in breathing). Absence of an obvious tachycardia (rapid pulse) is often strongly suggestive that the dyspnoea is non-cardiac in origin, although this is not always the case, especially in cats. Muffling of the heart sounds may be due to pleural or pericardial fluid, obesity, severe hypovolaemia (reduced circulating blood volume) or displacement of the heart by masses or other organs.

Disease or injury to upper airways usually results in loud dyspnoea, often with a prolonged inspiratory phase. Nasal disease may result in stertorous noises, while pharyngeal and laryngeal disorders result in stridorous breathing.

Sedation may help some cases – severe obstructions require immediate relief with trans-tracheal oxygen. Tracheostomy is always best performed as an elective procedure rather than as an emergency in a dying patient.

Pleural space disease

Although pleural space disease is often characterised by rapid shallow breathing with exaggerated abdominal movement, there may sometimes be surprisingly little outward indication.

The dorsal and ventral thorax should be auscultated on both sides; percussion may be useful to determine if fluid is present. Do not attempt to radiograph severely dyspnoeic patients and especially patients with suspected pleural space disease. Thoracocentesis is therapeutic (life-saving in tension pneumothorax) and often diagnostic in these cases. Equipment for thoracocentesis consists of:

• 20 ml syringe + stopcock + 20G needle (butterfly needle useful in cats).

Thoracocentesis is performed at the 6th to 8th intercostal space immediately cranial to the rib; the pleural cavity is tapped dorsally for air and ventrally for fluid. Local analgesia is rarely needed unless a large bore catheter is used for draining large volumes. If large volumes of air or fluid are being retrieved or a seal cannot be obtained, a chest drain is required. Numerous varieties of drain are available; placement can be performed under local analgesia, with the drain being tunnelled subcutaneously for 1–2 rib spaces before entering the chest. Patients with haemothorax should be managed without drainage unless the dyspnoea becomes too severe.

Patients with diaphragmatic rupture often have co-existing injuries (rib fractures, hypovolaemia, pulmonary contusions) and should not be taken to surgery unless stabilised first. Possible exceptions include gastrothorax or other situations where respiratory compromise is excessive. Not all diaphragmatic ruptures are radiographically obvious, and there can be a significant time tap between the injury and passage of abdominal viscera through the defect. The sudden deterioration of a trauma patient 24–72 hours post-admission should, therefore, prompt aggressive re-evaluation.

Flail chests occur when multiple fractures of adjacent ribs are present, resulting in a free-floating segment of chest wall that moves paradoxically with respiration. More recent experimental evaluation of this injury has shown that effects on deadspace and ventilation may not be as severe as was once thought; however, stabilisation may still be appropriate on analgesic grounds. This can be achieved simply by lying the patient on the affected side or by use of a rigid 'girdle' and circumcostal sutures if severe flail segments are present.

Bite wounds to the thoracic wall should always be treated as serious until proven otherwise, because the visible injury is very often only the 'tip of the iceberg' and extensive intercostal and costal damage, together with a pneumothorax, may exist beneath. Provision of a pleural seal and pleural drainage are the main priorities. Once the patient is stabilised, aggressive debridement and exploration are indicated.

Small airway disease

This often presents as laboured but not fast respiration. Expiratory wheezes and crackles may be present and, usually, a cough can be elicited (one of the few situations that may result in coughing in cats). Following oxygen therapy and initial stabilisation, radiographic evaluation is indicated together with cytological evaluation of airway secretions (harvested via bronchoscopy or trans-tracheal wash).

The following drugs may be useful in specific emergency therapy of asthmatic crisis or bronchospasm:

* terbutaline 0.01 mg per kg, slow intravenous (i.v.) delivery
* adrenaline 0.02 mg per kg, intramuscular (i.m.) delivery (in life-threatening cases)
* dexamethasone 0.5 mg per kg, i.v.
* theophylline 5 mg per kg, i.v. over one hour

Pulmonary parenchymal disease may be due to pulmonary contusions following trauma, infection resulting in pneumonias (particularly aspiration in patients with vomiting or regurgitation) or pulmonary oedema, which may be due to cardiac failure or non-cardiac causes (over hydration, head injury, seizures, electric shock, strangulation). Severe dyspnoea with soft cough and crackles on auscultation are often evident.

Assessment of oxygenation in dyspnoeic patients

Mucous membranes should always be examined, but are notoriously unreliable. Cyanosis (bluish tinge due to poor oxygenation of blood) can be masked by anaemia, poor perfusion or sepsis. Any doubt should prompt the rapid administration of oxygen until further clinical evaluation can be performed.

Pulse oximetry (measurement of the proportion of oxygenated haemoglobin) is non-invasive and easy to use, and provides useful information regarding peripheral perfusion and saturation, although poor probe compliance is often a problem. Dyspnoeic patients may also be peripherally vasoconstricted, reducing peripheral blood flow.

Arterial blood gas analysis is the gold standard for respiratory assessment, and provides information about oxygenation and ventilation. However, sampling may be technically difficult and the necessary equipment is expensive.

Oxygen supplementation

Oxygen should be given to all dyspnoeic patients immediately, even before any diagnostic attempts are made. This can be achieved in a variety of ways.

1 'Flow-by' oxygen involves simply placing the oxygen line or patient-end of an anaesthetic breathing system next to the patient's mouth and nose. It is simple and safe but not efficient.

2 Mask oxygen is probably the most commonly used method, but may create more stress if the animal resents the mask or if high fresh gas flows are used. Try and use masks that conform approximately to the shape of the patient's face; this eliminates significant deadspace and allows lower oxygen flows to be used.

3 Cage oxygen is expensive and oxygen can be lost when the door opens, but it probably remains the only way of giving oxygen in high inspired concentrations without intubation.

4 Human infant incubators are invaluable for smaller patients; they allow effective observation and can provide a non-invasive, well-oxygenated environment that can be warmed and humidified.

5 Crowe oxygen collar is an Elizabethan collar with clingfilm stretched over the front and a gap left at the top to prevent excessive humdification.

6 Nasal or nasopharyngeal routes are effective for longer term oxygen administration, but care should be taken not to distress the patient excessively during their placement. Nasopharyngeal tubes are pre-measured from the tip of the nose to the medial canthus and are inserted into the ventral nasal meatus following its desensitisation with topical local analgesic.

7 Endotracheal intubation and intermittent positive-pressure ventilation (IPPV) with 100% oxygen or oxygen-enriched air allows total control of ventilation and airway pressures, but represents a drastic step in terms of the level of patient care required (nursing, monitoring, sedation, paralysis, complications). However, electively anaesthetising a severely dyspnoeic patient in order to take control of ventilation is always superior to intubation and IPPV following a respiratory arrest.

Cardiovascular assessment

Take the heart rate and pulse rate (values may be different if there is an arrhythmia present). Pulse rhythm, quality and strength should also be assessed. Mucous membrane colour and capillary refill time should also be noted. Get secure intravenous access in all cases if possible.

Apply pressure to any obvious sites of bleeding; tourniquets are contra-indicated unless the limb is not salvageable, a decision best left to the clinician. Pressure distal to a limb wound helps to slow venous bleeding, while direct pressure and pressure proximal to a limb wound reduce arterial and local bleeding. Unexplained hypotension and shock are often due to intra-abdominal or retroperitoneal bleeding. This may be best controlled by using abdominal counter-pressure bandaging.

Before starting fluids, baseline blood and urine samples are required; taking blood after fluids have been started makes any subsequent laboratory information difficult to interpret.

Baseline samples should include:

- packed cell volume (PCV)
- total plasma proteins (TPP)
- electrolytes (sodium, potassium, chloride, calcium)
- glucose
- urea
- urinalysis
- fluid administration (see Chapter 4).

10

Patients with signs of severe hypovolaemia or poor tissue perfusion may require rapid fluid rates (60–90 ml per kg in the first hour). Some groups of critically ill patients may not tolerate large volumes of crystalloid fluid:

- animals with pulmonary parenchymal disease
- animals with ongoing haemorrhage
- animals with head injury
- animals with cardiac disease
- animals with severe anaemia.

These patients require more cautious rates of fluid administration and need careful monitoring to ensure that deterioration does not occur. Colloids given alone or with hypertonic saline may be effective in patients with head injury. Following initial stabilisation, the use of central venous pressure (CVP) to monitor fluid loading and response can be invaluable in the longer term; the normal range is 5–10 cmH$_2$O, measured using a water column manometer. The rate of decline of CVP after a fluid bolus is a useful guide to volume status; rapid declines or failure to rise indicate the continued presence of hypovolaemia.

If abnormal rhythm is suspected as a cause for the poor tissue perfusion, a lead II electrocardiogram (ECG) is required. Some patients need arrhythmia control to maintain adequate cardiac output.

Central nervous system assessment

The animal's level of consciousness should be assessed. A simple grading system can be used with a scale of 1 to 5 can be used:

- 5 (alert and responsive)
- 4 (depressed)
- 3 (severely depressed or delerium)
- 2 (stuporous but rousable)
- 1 (comatose; not rousable).

Other scoring systems are available.

Seizuring animals should be given oxygen immediately and attempts should be made to secure intravenous access (if it is not already present). Diazepam should be prepared and administered on the instruction of the attending clinician; if an intravenous route is not available, then the drug can be administered rectally or intranasally. Equipment for endotracheal intubation and IPPV should be prepared for use.

Further assessment of the nervous system need not be comprehensive at this stage and can be performed by nursing staff. Evaluation should consider:

- Is the animal recumbent?
- Can the animal walk?
- Is the gait normal or abnormal?
- Are there any signs of pain?

Definitive physical examination and further tests

Following major body system assessment and stabilisation, the opportunity should be taken to perform a more detailed assessment of the animal. This provides the clinician with an opportunity to decide on further diagnostic investigations, and o discuss subsequent action with the owner. This is also an appropriate time to assess the patient's response to primary therapy and make adjustments where indicated. A more detailed history can be obtained if necessary, and consent for any further procedures should be obtained or reconfirmed as appropriate.

2 Monitoring the critically ill patient

Regular, and often constant, monitoring forms the bulk of the nurse's role in critical care. After the initial evaluation of patient status, monitoring provides a means of continued re-assessment of the patient's condition as well as responses to therapy. The selection of parameters to be monitored (and the frequency with which they are monitored) depends on the nature of the clinical disease process, prior investigations and the results of the initial patient evaluation. The level of monitoring and type of equipment used depend on factors including equipment availability, operator experience and the need for accuracy. With repeated evaluations, the most important information is often provided by determining trends in vital signs. These trends may provide a better indication of patient response than the recording of accurate but infrequent measurements. It is, therefore, important that data is recorded in a readily accessible way allowing trends to be detected quickly. Use of a grid sheet and a 'join-the-dots' recording system (similar to anaesthetic monitoring) allows more rapid assessment of trends than columns of numbers. The key to effective patient monitoring is to anticipate changes, rather than to react when they occur.

Equipment

Purchase of equipment (particularly monitoring equipment) for use in the ICU carries with it the potential for significant expense, but it should be remembered that its use should be accounted for within the unit's pricing structure. Staff should be encouraged to read around the subject of equipment use. Ex-hospital suppliers and medical auction houses are good sources of new and used items. The maxim 'try before you buy' should be closely adhered to. Many excellent suppliers are now available and, consequently, prices are more competitive. It is worth purchasing monitoring equipment only if the personnel involved in its use are able to interpret the data that it provides; appropriate training of all staff involved in critical patient care is, therefore, important if finances are not to be squandered.

Organising patient monitoring

To ensure that patient evaluation is complete and vital checks and treatments are not omitted (or duplicated), a checklist of the necessary elements of patient monitoring should be adhered to. The frequency with which each element is assessed varies from patient to patient and is dictated by attending clinicians (in consultation with nursing staff). The following list may be suitable:

* airway, ventilation and oxygenation
* heart rate and rhythm
* tissue perfusion and pressures
* fluid requirements
* mental status and level of consciousness
* pain assessment and control
* urine output and specific gravity

- laboratory assessment
  - glucose
  - electrolytes
  - acid–base status
  - urea / creatinine
  - red blood cells (RBC) and white blood cells (WBC)
  - urinalysis
  - coagulation
- drugs and doses
- gut function and nutritional assessment
- dressings and indwelling catheters
- patient comfort.

Airway, ventilation and oxygenation

The patency and quality of the animal's airway should be checked. This particularly applies to patients with tracheostomy tubes in place, and to patients that are intubated and receiving IPPV. These patients should have the tube cuff deflated and gently repositioned every four hours to avoid pressure damage in the trachea.

Tracheostomy tubes require constant attention as occlusion can occur extremely rapidly, and patients cannot cough to clear the obstruction. The following guidelines are advisable for patients with indwelling tracheostomy.

1 The tube bypasses normal warming and humidification mechanisms. Instil 0.1 ml per kg of sterile saline down the tube (aseptically) every 2 hours (this may cause some coughing).

2 Suction is not a benign procedure and the patient should be pre-oxygenated for approximately 10 breaths prior to suctioning. the catheter should be aseptically introduced into the tube and suction applied for *no more than 15 seconds* as the suction tube is gently rotated. Suction may be required as often as every 15 minutes but should be performed at least four times daily. Some coughing, retching or gagging may be seen during suctioning. Ideally, a sterile catheter should be used each time but if this is not possible, the catheter should be flushed with sterile saline and changed daily.

3 The tracheostomy wound should be inspected daily and cleaned with sterile saline and swabs as necessary.

4 Tube changes may need to be done daily and should not be done in the absence of a clinician or facilities for endotracheal intubation and administration of oxygen. Pre-oxygenate the patient and grasp the stay sutures, applying gentle traction away from the wound. Remove the old tube and rapidly insert the new one. The assistance of a clinician should be sought if the following conditions arise:
  - severe dyspnoea – give 100% oxygen down tube or by mask if tube blocked
  - tube dislodged, blocked or removed – give oxygen
  - discharge from wound
  - any other concerns arise.

Equipment for respiratory monitoring includes pulse oximetry, respired gas analysis (most commonly capnography – end-expiratory carbon dioxide analysis) and blood gas analysis. Pulse oximeters are now widely available to the veterinary profession and are commonly used in anaesthetic monitoring. Potential applications in critical patient monitoring are equally suitable, but greater problems are encountered with maintaining good probe–patient contact and signal generation. Oximeters with a waveform-based indicator of pulse volume generally give more meaningful results, and many newer models contain software designed to eliminate movement artefact from the signal. It should be remembered that pulse oximeters only measure saturation, and tissue oxygen delivery relies on other factors as well, namely cardiac output and adequate haemoglobin concentrations.

Regular auscultation of the chest fields is important to detect any abnormal lung sounds suggesting fluid build-up or the development of pneumonia. The most accurate method of assessing the adequacy of patient oxygenation and ventilation is through arterial blood gas analysis. The necessary equipment is expensive, and accurate interpretation is important, but this method is essential if ventilated patients are to be managed successfully. On a simpler level, a reliable pulse oximeter reading of less than 90–95% (suggesting hypoxia), or any evidence of respiratory distress or cyanosis should prompt immediate oxygen supplementation. Hypoventilation (shallow or slow breathing) causing a build-up of carbon dioxide can also be detected using capnography. Patients with reduced consciousness, head injuries or other intracranial diseases may be at risk of hypoventilation.

Heart rate and rhythm

Bradycardia is slowness in the beating of the heart; tachycardia is rapid heartbeat. Heart rate can be monitored and measured by:

- simple palpation of the apex beat on the animal's chest wall
- palpation of peripheral or central arterial pulses
- direct auscultation with a stethoscope
- use of an electrocardiogram.

Severe bradycardias (less than 60 beats per minute in dogs o 100–140 bpm in cats) or tachycardias (more than 160 bpm in dogs or 220 bpm in cats) require investigation and rapid management. Arrhythmias are common in many forms of critical illness and may need specific therapy.

Use of an ECG allows specific diagnosis of any cardiac rhythm disturbance that might be present, but gives no information regarding cardiac output, tissue perfusion or arterial blood pressure. Units are either available as a stand-alone option or as part of a multi-function unit. Most machines possess a freeze facility that allows more detailed examination of the waveform.

Tissue perfusion and pressures

The essential function of the cardiovascular system is to adequately perfuse the tissues with oxygenated blood in order to maintain normal cellular metabolism. Abnormalities in cardiovascular function and tissue perfusion are common in patients with major illness and injury; regular monitoring is therefore essential to detect adverse trends early on.

Perfusion of tissues is indirectly assessed using a variety of means:

- peripheral pulse palpation
- mucous membrane colour and capillary refill time and vigour
- peripheral limb temperature / core temperature difference (less than 10 °F or 5.5 °C)
- urine output is a useful indicator of renal perfusion (less than 0.5 ml per kg per hour)
- adequacy of pulse oximeter signal
- patient's hydration status
- arterial blood pressure measurement.

A minimum mean arterial blood pressure of 60–70 mmHg (millimetres of mercury) is essential to maintain adequate blood flow to vital organs. This approximately equates to a systolic pressure of 90 mmHg, which can be measured more accurately than the mean pressure using indirect methods. Although invasive arterial pressure measurement represents the gold standard, arterial catheter placement can be technically difficult and the necessary transducers and monitors can be difficult to source. Non-invasive blood pressure measurement is less accurate, especially in hypotensive patients, but acceptable values can be obtained with instruments such as the Doppler system and oscillometric cuff-based systems. In order for accurate readings to be taken, the cuff width should be 40–60% of the limb circumference; therefore, a range of cuff sizes should be available.

Hypotension may be due to a number of causes; in every case, the patient's circulating volume status should be assessed first. Central venous pressure is an invaluable method of assessing the adequacy of circulating volume and should be monitored in hypotensive patients wherever possible (see Chapter 4).

Fluid requirements

The patient's fluid losses, normal maintenance fluid requirements (usually about 2 ml per kg per hour) and ongoing fluid losses should be assessed and replaced. Many critically ill patients with sepsis or systemic inflammatory responses will have 'leaky' capillaries, resulting in loss of fluid and albumin from the vascular space. Use of colloids such as hetastarch reduces the risk of crystalloid over-administration and helps to maintain intravascular volume. Oral fluids should be made available to patients able to drink.

Mental status and level of consciousness

The patient's level of consciousness should be regularly assessed and scored. This particularly applies to patients with head injuries or other intracranial disorders, or patients recovering from neurodiagnostic or neurosurgical procedures. Any behavioural changes should be noted. Seizures are an emergency and require immediate oxygen and anticonvulsant therapy. Always check blood glucose levels in patients with sudden neurological deterioration or seizures.

Pain assessment and control

Signs of pain or discomfort may be difficult to accurately assess in severely ill, very nervous or debilitated patients, but the nurses' or clinicians' inability to detect pain does not mean it is not present. Pain-associated signs in animals include:

- vocalisation (barking, growling, yelping – more common in dogs than cats)
- depression
- inappetance
- tachypnoea or panting
- pale mucous membranes
- tachycardia
- cardiac arrhythmias
- aggression
- abnormal postures including lameness
- restlessness (more often with visceral pain)
- hypotension
- hypertension
- hypersalivation
- mydriasis (dilated pupils).

Pre-emptive and multi-modal analgesic techniques should be used wherever possible. Opioids remain the drugs of choice for severe pain, and are suitable in critical patients due to their lack of cardiovascular effects. Non-steroidal anti-inflammatory drugs should be used with caution, as their potential side-effects on the gut and on renal blood flow are more likely in critically ill patients. This is less of an issue with the newer agents. Local analgesic techniques should be employed if possible.

Urine output and specific gravity

Urine output provides a useful indication of renal function and also fluid balance. Urine output should ideally be at least 1 ml per kg per hour in healthy patients. In recumbent patients, an indwelling urinary catheter should be aseptically placed and connected to a sterile closed collection system, as open urinary catheters predispose to urinary tract infection. All indwelling catheters and tubes should be inspected at least twice daily for signs of contamination or infection. Urine samples can be taken to assess urine specific gravity and to check for the presence of bacteria. Oliguria (less than 0.5 ml per kg per hour) suggests either an obstruction to urine flow, inadequate renal blood flow or primary acute renal dysfunction, and should be investigated. Further fluid therapy or diuretic management may be indicated.

Laboratory assessment

The frequency and nature of laboratory-based assessment are determined by the severity and nature of the patient's underlying disease.

Glucose

Ideally, blood glucose concentrations should be maintained at 5–8 mmol per litre. Hypoglycaemia (reduced blood glucose level) may occur with conditions such as seizures, sepsis and sever liver disease, and supplementation of intravenous fluid may be required. Persistent glucosuria (glucose in the urine), as a result of unstable diabetes mellitus or iatrogenic glucose administration, may predispose to urinary tract infection.

Electrolytes

Sodium, potassium and calcium should be maintained within normal limits. Hypokalaemia (reduced blood potassium level) is common in inappetant patients receiving fluid therapy, and the response to supplementation should be monitored carefully.

Acid–base status

Metabolic acidosis is a common sequel to poor tissue perfusion, and arterial or venous blood gas analysis is useful to determine the severity of the problem. Specific therapy is not often required for acid–base disorders, but monitoring of status and response to treatment is useful in severe disorders. Sodium bicarbonate is commonly used to treat metabolic acidosis (but is contra-indicated in respiratory acidosis), and should not be mixed with calcium-containing fluids.

Urea / creatinine

Further assessment of renal function is provided by these tests. In patients with severe renal failure, regular daily monitoring of urea and creatinine (together with urine output) provides a guide to the patient's response to therapy. Gastrointestinal bleeding causes mild to moderate elevations in urea.

RBC and WBC

Haemodilution may occur in patients receiving large fluid volumes, especially if previous haemorrhage or haemolysis has occurred. The optimal haematocrit for efficient oxygen transport is 27–33% (corresponds to a haemoglobin concentration of 9–11 g per dl); red cell, whole blood or haemoglobin replacement may be necessary in some patients to maintain this level. The white blood cell counts give a broad indication of the presence of infectious or inflammatory disease; a sudden rise or marked fall in levels should prompt an aggressive search for a focus of infection, particularly in animals on large doses of corticosteroids.

Urinalysis

Urine specific gravity should be assessed daily. Urine should also be evaluated for the presence of blood, glucose, bacteria and casts, which may indicate renal tubular damage.

Coagulation

Coagulopathy, in the form of disseminated intravascular coagulation (DIC), is a common sequel to major trauma and many diseases causing critical illness. All patients in the ICU should be regularly and aggressively assessed for signs of altered haemostasis, which may include:

- petechial haemorrhages on mucous membranes
- haematoma or persistent bleeding after surgery, blood sampling or catheterisation

- subcutaneous bruising
- low platelet count
- altered clotting times.

Patients with diseases associated with haemostatic disorders should have their coagulation assessed on admission to ICU and regularly thereafter. Therapy of DIC is difficult and expensive, and may require aggressive haemodynamic support, fresh whole blood or fresh plasma transfusions, and heparin therapy. Heparinisation may also be needed in animals at risk of thromboembolic disease.

Drugs and doses

The need for drug therapy in critical patients is usually high, but needs to be continually re-assessed in light of the patient's response to treatment, side-effects and interactions of drugs used, and existence of conditions that may affect drug metabolism and excretion. Hepatic or renal dysfunction may prolong or potentiate drug action, and doses may need to be adjusted. Infection is common in critical illness, and antibiotic selection should, ideally, be based on results of culture and sensitivity tests on fluid, blood or tissue samples. Combinations of intravenous antibiotics may be required in sepsis or severe infections.

Gut function and nutritional assessment

Abdominal auscultation should be performed regularly to determine the presence and frequency of gut sounds. Gut stasis predisposes the patient to vomiting and gut ulceration; prokinetic drugs may be required to promote intestinal motility. Any new vomiting or diarrhoea should be investigated. The presence of blood in vomit or faeces should prompt anti-ulcer therapy. Anti-emetic drugs are essential in vomiting patients that are depressed or recumbent, as the risk of aspiration is high.

Bodyweight and body condition should be assessed daily, and food intake monitored and increased accordingly. The use of parenteral nutrition should be considered in animals unable to meets protein-energy requirements by the oral route (see Chapter 3).

Dressings and indwelling catheters

Breaches in the skin surface are often the first sites where infection may localise in critically ill patients. Temperature should be taken every four hours and all dressings, bandages and indwelling tubing (intravascular cannulae, urinary catheters, wound or thoracic drains, feeding tubes) should be inspected at least twice daily for signs of infection. All such items should be placed, applied and handled aseptically; the importance of hand-washing and other aseptic measures between patients, and in the ICU in general, cannot be over-emphasised. Signs of infection around indwelling tubing include:

- heat, pain or swelling at site
- infusion failure
- hard tender vessel
- fever or high WBC count.

Intravascular cannulae should be removed if they are no longer functional, no longer required or are causing the patient distress. Dressings that have soaked through or are soiled with fluids should be replaced as soon as possible to avoid wound contamination. Patients with peritonitis that are undergoing open abdominal drainage may need abdominal dressings changed on an hourly basis in the early stages.

Patient comfort

All animals may find the ICU environment strange and distressing. Most patients are treasured pets, and are used to social contact and tender loving care from their owners. Every effort should be made to maintain good social contact, and the continued application of 'TLC' is vital to patient well-being.

Recumbent patients must be turned regularly (at least every four hours) to prevent decubital ulceration; passive limb movements should be performed to encourage blood flow. Paraplegic and post-orthopaedic patients benefit from more intensive physiotherapy.

Unconscious patients should be handled gently. The mouth, tongue and oral mucous membranes must be kept moist and clean with dilute chlorhexidine mouthwash daily. Bland topical ophthalmic ointments should be applied to both eyes to prevent corneal desiccation. Any damp bedding should be immediately changed; incontinence sheets or nappies can be useful to prevent excessive laundry loads, and can be weighed to assess urine output. Gentle bladder expression may be required in some patients. Faecal constipation may also be a problem, and warm saline enemas may be indicated.

All recumbent or immobile patients are at risk of the following complications:

- decubital ulceration over bony prominences
- dependent lung atelectasis (collapse of part of the lung) and hypostatic pneumonia
- muscular and ligamentous contracture and stiffening
- regional oedema (accumulation of fluid) as a result of poor lymphatic drainage or venous obstruction.

The following precautionary measures should be applied to prevent or minimise these problems:

- ensure the trunk and all appendages are positioned comfortably and reposition every four hours
- ensure good all-round padding
- prevent limbs from hanging over the edge of cots or tables
- put patients (especially ventilated patients) in sternal recumbency wherever possible.

3 Nutritional support

Provision of adequate nutritional requirements is essential in patients with major illness and injury, and has been shown to have significant impact on morbidity and mortality. A wide variety of diets is available to facilitate effective nutrition in these patients, but a good working knowledge of the pathophysiology of malnutrition and the clinical techniques used in nutritional support is also important.

Effects of food deprivation

In the fit, healthy patient, deprivation of food (known commonly as simple starvation) results in a down-regulation of metabolism via neurohumoral mechanisms and a conservation of energy stores, with lipid dominating as the principal substrate for metabolism. This process is assisted by an overall reduction in physical activity, facilitating energy conservation.

In a patient with significant disease or injury (stressed starvation) neuro-endocrine and humoral mechanisms result in a hypermetabolic and catabolic state, resulting in overriding of protective responses. This leads to an increase in nutrient requirements, but with altered utilisation. In absence of food intake, all body systems will ultimately be affected (Figure 2). However, before affecting other body systems, major effects are seen in the gastrointestinal tract. The small intestine is one of the most metabolically active organs in the body, and derives a significant amount of its nutrition at a local level directly from the gut lumen.

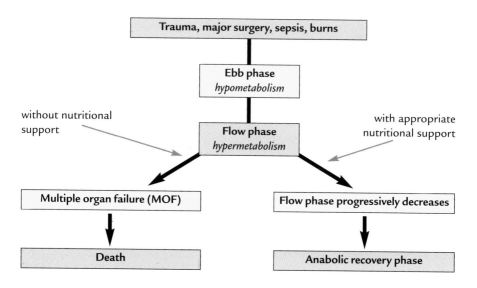

Figure 2   Flow of events in intensive care

Failure to feed leads to:

- loss of brush border enzymes
- loss of nutrient transport
- mucosal and villous atrophy
- loss of gut-associated lymphoid tissue
- alterations in gut flora.

These changes allow bacterial translocation, resulting in the potential passage of enteric bacteria and endotoxins across the gut mucosa. The liver cannot clear this massive load of toxins in the usual manner; thus the gut can potentially act as a source of secondary infection and sepsis in the malnourished critically ill or injured patient.

Other major systemic changes resulting from stressed starvation include reduced white cell function, depression of immune function, reduced tissue synthesis and delayed wound healing, and derangement of drug metabolism.

When should nutritional support be instituted?

Many available guidelines are derived from human nutritional studies and are inappropriate. Three to five days of real or anticipated anorexia in veterinary species is the acceptable limit in simple starvation. In stressed starvation, the need for adequate protein-energy nutrition is much more urgent and metabolic scaling also suggests that the smaller the patient and the more severe the disease, the sooner nutritional support should be started. The maxim 'they don't eat when they feel better, they feel better when they eat' should be well remembered.

Assessing nutritional status

Numerous methods and biochemical markers have been proposed as accurate markers of a patient's nutritional status. In many instances it is difficult to separate the effects of disease from the effects of malnutrition, and tests of muscular strength and height–weight scaling are obviously inappropriate in veterinary species. Consequently, a system described in humans as subjective global assessment (essentially a thorough history, body condition scoring and physical examination) has become the most popular way of evaluating patients.

Historical findings that should prompt urgent nutritional support include:

- acute weight loss of more than 5% expected body weight
- chronic weight loss of more than 10% expected body weight
- more than three days of anorexia or inappetance.

Physical findings that should prompt urgent nutritional support include:

- poor body condition (cachexia)
- musculoskeletal atrophy
- major trauma
- non-healing or infected wounds.

Body condition scoring involves evaluation of body composition:

1 very thin

2 underweight

3 ideal weight

4 overweight

5 obese.

Many scales are used, but most systems involve evaluation and palpation of the abdomen, ribs, pelvic bony landmarks and base of the tail.

Assessing nutritional requirements

Caloric requirements

Historically, caloric requirements were derived from the product of a calculated basal energy requirement (BER) and an illness factor that increased in proportion to the severity of disease or injury. This is now thought to be excessive, and caloric needs are possibly not that great. Required caloric levels are now usually based on a calculated resting energy requirement (RER), which is 10–20% greater than BER. Excessive feeding may result in gastrointestinal disturbances and, in patients receiving respiratory support or ventilation, may result in excessive levels of carbon dioxide production and failure to wean off ventilation.

Basal energy requirement – expenditure in a healthy animal lying at rest 12 hours after feeding, under no stress and in a thermoneutral environment.

Resting energy requirement – expenditure in a healthy animal undergoing mild activity 12 hours after feeding, under no stress and in a thermoneutral environment.

Calculating RER

Energy requirements, including RER, in species with large differences in body weight (such as dogs) are not related to body weight but to metabolic weight ($kg^{0.75}$). If calculated per kilogram of body weight, small dogs (2.5 kg) would need about twice as many calories as large dogs (60 kg).

In all patients (dogs and cats) the following formula can be used:

$RER = 70$ kcal/$kg^{0.75}$

Alternative methods of calculating RER

In cats, the following alternative equation can be used:

$RER = 50$ kcal/kg (of body weight)

In dogs, the following alternative equation can be used:

$RER = (30 \times$ body weight in kg$) + 70$

However, the alternative formula for dogs underestimates the energy requirements in small dogs (≤ 5 kg) and overestimates RER in large dogs (≥ 30 kg).

Protein requirements

Although energy requirements may have previously been overestimated by clinicians, protein requirements in critical care patients are commonly underestimated. Because of their catabolic state and potential carbohydrate intolerance, energy for critical care patients should mainly come from fat and protein. In addition, certain amino acids (e.g. glutamine, branched chain amino acids, and arginine) are needed in higher proportions than usual. The protein requirements of dogs thus become similar to those of cats. Cats can not down-regulate their protein metabolism because of their specific requirements for energy production and nitrogen.

Branched chain amino acids help to replenish those that are used in higher amounts in gluconeogenesis (the process by which the body changes pyruvic acid to glucose) and to slow down muscle atrophy. Arginine helps to stimulate the anabolic phase of metabolism and to detoxify the ammonia generated by intensive protein metabolism.

Glutamine is an important substrate in nutritional support. It is the most abundant amino acid in the body but in conditions of critical illness, demand often outstrips supply and it may become conditionally essential. Glutamine acts as the primary energy substrate for the gut and plays an important role in gut metabolism and immunity. It also acts as an energy source for macrophages and lymphocytes. Requirements are increased in the presence of infection and a net uptake of glutamine occurs from the lung in major disease and sepsis. There is some evidence that feeding glutamine-supplemented parenteral diets results in increased survival in critical illness; whether this effect can be achieved with supplementation of enteral diets is yet to be conclusively established.

In critical care patients (both dogs and cats), protein should provide at least 30% of energy requirements and should come from specific sources that are rich in arginine, glutamine and branched chain amino acids. Milk products are generally considered to be high-quality protein, but are low in arginine and should not, therefore, be the primary source.

Most animals tolerate well the high fat and protein levels of a critical care diet. However, patients with severe hepatic disease may not tolerate the high level of protein because of the increased amounts of ammonia and other protein-breakdown products that are generated. In such cases, a low-protein diet could be used. But before switching to a low-protein diet, consider that most critical care patients eat less food than usual unless they are tube fed. This means that (unless the animal is tube fed) a high-protein diet might still be the best option because the intake of protein is in fact relatively low due to the low food intake. As the intake is spread over several small meals, the risk of hepatic encephalopathy etc. is reduced. Moreover, the risk of underfeeding is less on a high-protein rather than a low-protein diet.

Some additional therapy (lactulose, oral antibiotics) to offset potential complications such as hepatic encephalopathy may also help. Similarly, patients in renal failure may need extra fluid diuresis in order to help eliminate increased amounts of urea.

Micronutrient requirements

Trace elements, other minerals, vitamins, fatty acids and other compounds make up this category. The effect of critical illness on their availability, storage and utilisation is uncertain, although most body stores may take some time to become depleted. Some vitamins, particularly the water-soluble ones, can become rapidly depleted, especially in polyuric patients or those on high fluid rates. Major electrolyte deficiencies can occur with malnutrition but are often more easily dealt with by alteration of the patient's fluid therapy regime.

How can the food be given?

Enteral nutrition

If the gut works, use it!

Enteral nutrition is generally cheaper and simpler than parenteral feeding, and maintains mucosal integrity more effectively. This reduces the likelihood of bacterial translocation and sepsis, and in comparative studies enteral nutrition has been shown to reduce morbidity and mortality more effectively than parenteral nutrition. Methods of enteral feeding include:

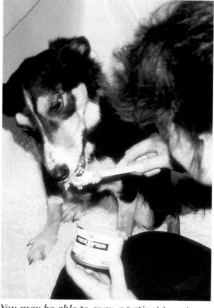

- chemical stimulation of appetite
- tube feeding
    - naso-oesophageal
    - pharyngostomy
    - oesophagostomy
    - gastrostomy
    - enterostomy.

You may be able to coax a patient to eat

Chemical stimulation of appetite

Chemical stimulation of appetite is often useful and should be considered in all patients who are not severely malnourished and have no physical reason for an inability to ingest food. The most commonly used drug in the acute situation is diazepam (0.05–0.1 mg per kg). Care should be exercised with long-term (more than 4–5 days) use of oral diazepam for this purpose in cats, as hepatotoxicity has been described. Low doses of propofol also have an appetite-stimulating effect, but this phenomenon is not well-investigated in veterinary patients. On a more chronic basis, appetite stimulation with anabolic steroids such as nandrolone or serotonin antagonists such as cyproheptadine may be useful.

Tube feeding

Which tube should be used? As proximal (i.e. close to the mouth) a point of entry to the gut as possible should be used. Factors affecting tube choice include:

- patient size – small patients need small tubes
- duration of feeding – nasal tubes are suitable for short-term feeding only

- disease or injury – for example, nasal tubes are contra-indicated in facial injuries
- expense – generally increases the further down the gut the tube is placed
- vet or nurse familiarity with tube placement and care.

It should be remembered that in all tube feeding methods where the point of tube insertion is proximal to the stomach, the end of the tube should reside in the distal oesophagus and not pass through into the stomach. Entry of the tube into the stomach can provoke gastro-oesophageal reflux and tube regurgitation.

Naso-oesophageal tubes

Naso-oesophageal tubes are the tubes of choice for short-term feeding (10–14 days) and usually cause minimal complications. Placement can be performed in the conscious patient, which allows stabilisation prior to general anaesthetic (GA) and surgery. The small tube size means liquid diets must be used. These tubes are contra-indicated in patients with facial or nasal trauma, persistent vomiting or recumbent patients prone to aspiration. Human paediatric oesophageal tubes are suitable and widely available. Complications following placement are few, but can include vomiting and regurgitation, and a mild rhinitis, which usually resolves on tube removal. Place the tube using the following guidelines.

1 Measure and mark the tube, measuring nose to rib 9 or nose to last rib, and use 75% of this length.

2 Desensitise nose using several drops of proxymetacaine (Ophthaine) and sedate if required.

3 Lubricate and introduce the tube; aim ventromedially (toward base of opposite ear). In dogs, the nasal planum can

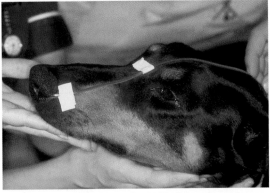

Naso-oesophageal tube in place in a dog

Above and above right: Naso-oesophageal tube in place in a cat

be pushed dorsally to direct the tube ventrally. Hold head in a normal position as tube enters pharynx to prevent tracheal intubation.

4 Check placement; 5–10 ml of water followed by the same volume of air should produce some bubbling sounds over the left flank, together with an absence of coughing. Radiography can also be used.

5 Secure tube over midline of the head: either suture or superglue and place an Elizabethan collar.

Pharyngostomy tubes

Pharyngostomy tubes require surgical placement similar to that required for oesophagostomy (exit point is through the caudal pharynx just behind the hyoid apparatus) but larger tubes can be used (Figure 3). This means more normal diets can be liquidised and used. The tube is suitable for short- to medium-term feeding but should not be used in small patients (less than 10 kg) as the tube can impinge on the larynx and affect laryngeal function, which may lead to aspiration pneumonia.

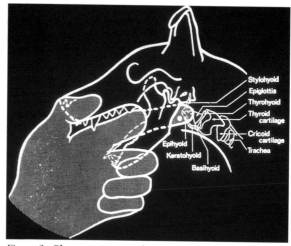

Figure 3   Pharyngostomy technique (courtesy of Dr Steve Crane)

Oesophagostomy tubes

Oesophagostomy tubes are suitable for longer-term support and have been maintained successfully for 3–4 months. Under heavy sedation or GA in right lateral recumbency, curved artery forceps are passed into the oesophagus and turned out laterally in the left mid-cervical region. A cut-down is made at this point and the pre-measured tube is inserted and sutured to the skin. The site should be carefully cleaned daily and a dressing applied. Flush tubes with warm water

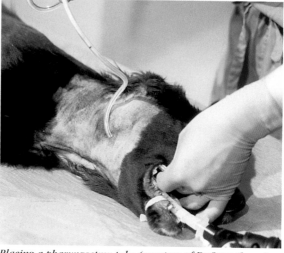

Placing a pharyngostmy tube (courtesy of Dr Steve Crane)

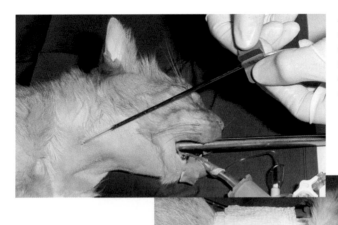

Left and below: Placing a oesophagostomy tube with the aid of a special device (courtesy of Dr J Robben, Utrecht University)

Below: A cat with an oesphagus tube in place can also eat independently (courtesy of Dr J Robben, Utrecht University)

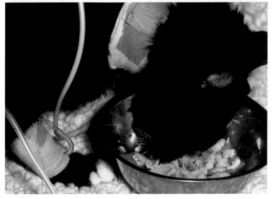

after each feed. These tubes have been maintained in both cats and dogs for several months with negligible complications. If the patient also has a jugular catheter in place, ensure that both tube and catheter are clearly labelled as such.

Commercial oesophagostomy tube-placement systems are available with an introducer and 'peel-away' sheath technique. These systems greatly facilitate tube placement.

Gastrostomy tubes

Gastrostomy tubes are probably the tubes of choice for patients requiring feeding for more than 10–14 days (and have been maintained for years) or patients with major oesophageal disease or dysfunction. Endoscopic (percutaneous endoscopic gastrostomy), surgical or 'blind' placement techniques are used. The following description relates to endoscopic placement; blind placement works along similar principles, but a rigid introducer is used to allow retrieval of a wire passed into the stomach percutaneously.

1 With the animal under general anaesthesia and in right lateral recumbency, an area on the left flank immediately caudal to the last rib is aseptically prepared.

2 The endoscope is inserted into the stomach via the mouth, and the stomach is inflated to aid visualisation and displace other viscera away from the site of tube insertion.

3 An assistant depresses the skin immediately caudal to the last rib and the site of indentation is detected endoscopically.

4 The assistant then passes a large bore needle (14–16G, 2") through the body wall at this site until it penetrates the gastric wall. A long flexible wire or heavy suture material is threaded through the needle and grasped using endoscopic forceps or a snare (Figure 4). The wire or suture is then pulled through into the stomach and drawn up the oesophagus and out through the mouth as the endoscope is withdrawn.

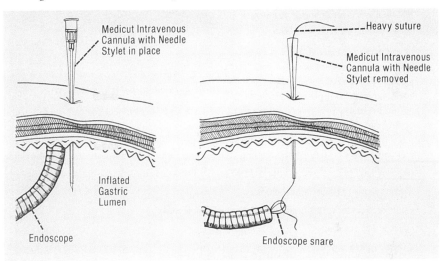

5 The feeding tube is then attached by its external end (i.e. not the mushroom) to the wire. Some tube systems have a conical end with a pre-attached wire loop to facilitate placement; otherwise a pipette tip or large intravenous catheter will suffice. The wire or suture is threaded through the tip of the catheter and then secured to the end of the tube.

6 The wire or suture is then withdrawn back into the stomach, pulling the tube behind it

Figure 4   Percutaneous gastronomy tube placement using an endoscope

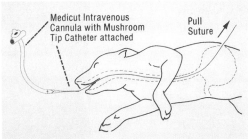

Figure 5   Gastronomy tube placement

(Figure 5). The catheter or pipette tip acts as a dilator, enlarging the hole in the body and stomach walls to allow passage of the tube.

7 The wire or suture is withdrawn until the bulk of the gastrostomy tube is outside the body wall, causing the mushroom tip to 'sandwich' the gastric and abdominal walls together (Figure 6). The external portion of the tube is then secured to the skin with a butterfly or finger-trap suture, preventing tube migration.

8 A sterile dressing is applied to the skin stoma site and the tube is flushed with sterile water. Feeding can commence after 24 hours.

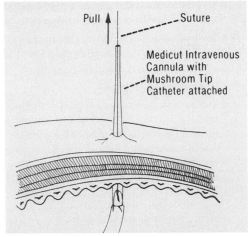

Figure 6 *The mushroom tip will sandwich the gastric and abdominal walls together*

For endoscopic placement, a 14–24 Fr mushroom-tip catheter is most commonly used; Foley catheters should be avoided if possible as the balloon invariably perishes, resulting in tube failure and possible leakage leading to peritonitis. Feeding can commence after 24 hours have allowed a primary seal to form. The tubes should be left in for 7–10 days to allow a good stoma to form. Removal is usually done endoscopically or in some cases cutting off the feeding adapter and pulling the tube out through the flank. The mushroom end is passed in the faeces.

Complications of placement include:

* splenic laceration or penetration (not always detected)
* gastric haemorrhage
* pneumoperitoneum
* vomiting or gulping – usually as a result of too rapid feeding
* delayed gastric emptying – more common in dogs than cats
* blockage – flush after feeds with clean water; carbonated drinks can be used to clear blocked tubes
* tube migration – regular checks to ensure correct position is maintained
* peritonitis
* stoma cellulitis – usually resolves after tube removal.

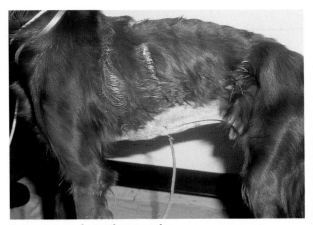

Enterostomy tube in place in a dog

Enterostomy tubes

Duodenostomy and jejunostomy tubes are available for veterinary use. They can be useful in cranial gastro-intestinal (GI) pathology and pancreatitis cases where introduction of nutrients into the lower small intestine supposedly prevents pancreatic activation and secretion. A mini-laparotomy is needed to place the tube, although some techniques allow endoscopic placement via a gastrostomy tube. Complications include tube displacement, blockage and GI disturbances due to the use of hyperosmolar and over-complex diets.

Which diet should be used?

Many diets specifically formulated for post-surgical and intensive care patients are widely available in the veterinary market (Table 1). However, one of the major factors influencing choice of food is tube type and size. Big tubes allow normal liquidised ('blenderised') diets to be fed; tubes with a diameter smaller than 8 Fr (and especially tubes with a side-hole) tend to block unless proprietary liquid diets are used.

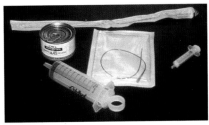

Hill's* Prescription Diet* canine/feline a/d* and feeding equipment

Numerous human liquid diets are available; these are not always correctly formulated for veterinary patients and are often too calorific. The wide range of veterinary-specific diets also makes the use of human diets questionable.

Table 1 Comparison of diets for post-surgical and intensive care patients

Diet	Caloric density (kcal per ml)	Protein (% of kcal)	Fat (% of kcal)	Carbohydrate (% of kcal)	Minimum tube size (Fr)
Hill's* Prescription Diet* Canine/Feline a/d* canned	1.3	34	53	13	8
Waltham® Canine Convalescence Support™ canned	1.4	28	47	24	6–8
Waltham® Canine Convalescence Support™ powder	1.4	37	39	24	8
Waltham® Feline Convalescence Support™ pouch	1.1	24	56	20	6–8
Waltham® Feline Convalescence Support™ pouch	1.2	34	50	16	8
Eukanuba® High Calorie Formula™ for Dogs canned	2.0	29	66	5	8
Eukanuba® High Calorie Formula™ for Cats canned	2.0	29	66	5	8

*Trademarks owned by Hill's Pet Nutrition, Inc.© 2003 Hill's Pet Nutrition, Inc.

Commercially available liquid or semi-liquid diets are more convenient and also allow the use of constant rate infusion (CRI) feeds. Of these products, Hill's* Prescription Diet* Canine/Feline a/d* was the first small animal critical-care product developed. It is a thixotropic paste (becomes semi-liquid on stirring) to permit easy dilution for tube feeding and to minimise the risk of accidental aspiration in very weak patients undergoing assisted feeding.

CRI feeding may offer advantages over bolus feeding in patients that have been anorexic for several days, namely by reducing the major gastrointestinal and electrolyte disturbances that can occur in these patients when feeding is resumed after a prolonged period of starvation. CRI feeding may be less useful in dogs, as anecdotal evidence suggests it may inhibit their normal pattern of gastrointestinal motility.

As a general rule, one-third to one-half of the calculated requirement should be fed on the first day and this should be divided between four to six feeds. Dilute the first feed 50 : 50 with warm water. If this is tolerated, the full amount can be gradually added over the next 24–48 hours. Always warm feeds to above room temperature and feed slowly. Tubes should always be flushed with clean water before and after every feed.

Parenteral nutrition

In patients with severely damaged or diseased gastrointestinal systems, where normal absorptive mechanisms are compromised, parenteral nutrition (PN) should be considered. The list of potential complications of PN is long, and patients receiving PN need 24-hour monitoring and assessment. PN solutions are also time-consuming to prepare (although newer composite preparations reduce this problem) and can be expensive. Careful thought and preparation are, therefore, needed before embarking on a PN regime in any patient.

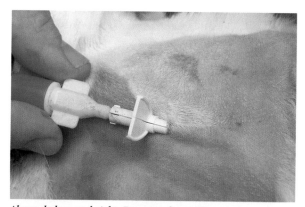

Above, below and right: Parenteral nutrition

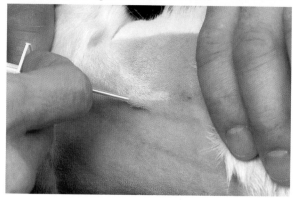

Intravenous access for PN should be dedicated: the line should be aseptically placed and should not be used for blood samples or drug administration. Central lines are traditionally used for PN due to the high osmolarity of the solutions used, but solutions of less than 500 mosmol per litre can be given through a peripheral vein without causing major thrombophlebitis. Polyurethane or silicone catheters provide the lowest risk for thrombophlebitis.

PN solutions are invariably a mixture of amino acid solutions, glucose and a lipid emulsion. Various micronutrients can be added, but as PN is usually a short-term measure (less than one week) in veterinary patients, this is not always essential. Solutions need to be prepared on a daily basis and under strict aseptic conditions. Many mineral and electrolyte solutions are not compatible with each other or with lipids, and care should be taken to avoid precipitation.

More recently, ready-formulated compound parenteral nutritional products (e.g. Kabiven®; Fresenius) have been evaluated in dogs; the results are promising. These preparations consist of compartmentalised infusion bags, which are compressed and rolled immediately prior to use in order to mix the separate substrates (lipid, amino acid, dextrose). Osmolarity is in the region of 500 mosmol per litre, which makes the solutions suitable for short-term peripheral venous use. The majority of these products are not licensed for veterinary use.

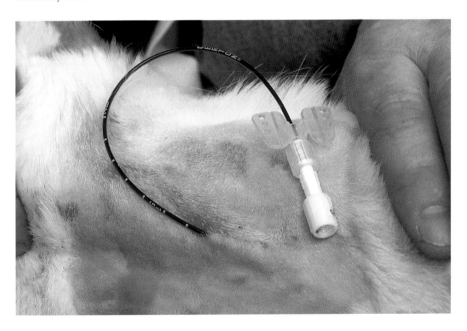

4 Fluid therapy

Many different diseases result in major imbalances of body fluids and electrolytes. Fluid therapy manages these disturbances while the underlying cause of the patient's illness or injury is identified and treated. Provided that the patient's renal and cardiac function are adequate, normal physiologic regulation ensures that there is a substantial margin for error in fluid therapy. In view of the difficulty encountered in making accurate assessments of fluid losses, this is quite fortunate.

Irrespective of whether the patient has just been admitted or has been hospitalised for some time, planning a fluid therapy regime should follow the same guidelines; ones similar to those suggested by DiBartola (2001) are eminently applicable:

- Does the patient (still) need fluid therapy?
- What type(s) of fluid does the patient need?
- By what route can this be given?
- How much fluid and how fast?
- When should fluid therapy be stopped?

Does the patient (still) need fluid therapy?

Indications for fluid therapy are as follows:

- historical, physical or laboratory-based evidence of fluid losses or reduced tissue perfusion
- administration of normal maintenance fluid and electrolyte requirements and any ongoing fluid losses
- haemodynamic support and maintenance of tissue perfusion during anaesthesia and surgery
- maintenance of venous access (for drugs, parenteral nutritional support).

The first of these bullet points is discussed in detail in the rest of this chapter.

Historical assessment of fluid losses

Always try to assess the severity of the losses and the time period over which fluid has been lost. Questions to be asked should include:

- Food and water consumption? (normal maintenance intake)
- Any vomiting or diarrhoea? (gastrointestinal losses)
- Any excessive or reduced urination? (urinary losses)
- Any blood loss or burns? (traumatic losses)

- Any pyrexia, excessive panting? (insensible losses)
- Any abdominal distension or dyspnoea? ('third space' losses e.g. ascites, pleural effusion).

Physical assessment of fluid losses

Physical findings associated with a fluid deficit will vary according to a number of factors:

- type of fluid lost
- speed of loss
- volume of fluid lost
- the patient's individual characteristics.

When examining patients, it is important to make the distinction between clinical signs associated with dehydration and those associated with hypoperfusion, although some patients may exhibit both.

Dehydration essentially means a loss from the free water content of the body but the term is commonly used to describe combined water and solute losses. It is fair to say that dehydration will lead to hypovolaemia if left untreated, but the two terms should not be used interchangeably. Patients with *dehydration* generally require more cautious fluid and electrolyte replenishment to replace body fluid losses. Patients with *reduced tissue perfusion* require rapid effective circulating volume replacement in order to avoid the effects of reduced organ blood flow and prolonged vasoconstriction. In the emergency patient, the latter state is a primary concern. Once perfusion status is restored, or if perfusion is adequate, then fluid and electrolyte status can be determined via assessment of historical, physical and laboratory-based findings.

Clinical signs associated with *dehydration* include:

- reduced skin turgor and pliability
- dry or tacky mucous membranes
- eyes sunken within orbit
- reduced alertness
- muscular weakness.

It should be remembered that obese animals and neonates often have good skin turgor even when hydrated (due to high levels of subcutaneous fat), and elderly or cachectic animals often have poor skin turgor in spite of good hydration status.

Signs of poor *tissue perfusion include*:

- tachycardia
- rapid weakened pulse
- cool extremities
- prolonged capillary refill (may be shortened in sepsis)
- pale mucous membranes (may be injected in sepsis)
- dull mental status.

If the onset of the hypoperfusion is acute, the classical signs of dehydration will not have had time to develop and will not be present.

Measurement or estimation of body weight should always form part of the physical examination, as fluid losses impact on bodyweight (one litre of body fluid weighs one kilogram). Patients experiencing 'third-space' fluid losses (i.e. into a body cavity or hollow organ) do not lose weight.

Laboratory assessment of fluid losses

It is essential that any blood or urine samples taken as primary assessment should be taken before commencing fluid therapy, so that a baseline for monitoring subsequent trends can be easily established. Measurement of packed cell volume (PCV), total plasma proteins (TPP) and urine specific gravity (USG) usually form a part of any patient laboratory database and these values can be assessed to give some indication of the type and volume of fluid lost. PCV and TPP should be assessed together, as their relative proportions are affected by different types of loss (Table 2). The effects of any underlying disease on the patient's values should be borne in mind. The USG should be high in a dehydrated animal with normal kidney function.

Table 2   Differential diagnosis based on relative proportions of PCV and TPP

PCV	TPP	Differential diagnosis
Increased	increased	• dehydration
	normal	• splenic contraction
		• primary or secondary polycythaemia
		• haemorrhagic gastroenteritis (very high PCV)
Normal	normal	• normal
		• dehydration with hypoproteinaemia
		• anaemia with hypoproteinaemia and dehydration
	decreased	• recent haemorrhage (mild)
		• liver disease
		• protein losing nephropathy or enteropathy
		• third-space protein loss
Decreased	normal	• haemolysis
		• decreased red cell production
		• chronic low-grade haemorrhage
	decreased	• haemorrhage (acute)

What type(s) of fluid does the patient need?

A diverse range of fluid products is available and selection should be made on the basis of specific indications as with any other drug. The three main groups are crystalloids, colloids and blood products.

Crystalloids

Crystalloids are composed of water, electrolytes and/or glucose. These fluids distribute freely within all the fluid compartments, largely according to their tonicity. Crystalloids are most conveniently classified as either replacement or maintenance solutions according to their composition.

Replacement solutions are all essentially isotonic and sodium-based – they are like extracelluar fluid (ECF). The three main isotonic replacement crystalloids in regular veterinary use in the UK are Ringers, Hartmann's (lactated Ringer's),and normal (0.9%) saline. These equilibrate with the interstitial space and, therefore, only 20–25% of any volume given remains in the vasculature following redistribution, which means that large volumes may often be required to manage severe hypovolaemia.

Replacement solutions can be further classified as alkalinising or acidifying depending on their effect on plasma pH. Normal saline has a sodium content similar to plasma but acts as an 'acidifying' solution. The mechanisms for this are threefold:

• dilution of plasma bicarbonate

• reduction of bicarbonate absorption within kidney

• promotion of bicarbonate secretion in collecting tubules in the kidney.

Normal saline is also the fluid of choice for diuresis in patients with hypercalcaemia (raised blood calcium level) due to the effects of increased calcium filtration and reduced calcium reabsorption within the kidney. Hartmann's and Ringer's contain calcium, which may be incompatible with some additives such as bicarbonate.

Maintenance solutions (5% dextrose in water (D5W); 0.18% saline + 4% glucose) are low-sodium, glucose-based solutions. The glucose content is not calorifically significant (a 10 kg dog would need four litres of 5% glucose a day in order to satisfy its daily maintenance energy requirement) and such fluids are not suitable for ECF expansion as less than 10% remains in the intravascular space following redistribution. Rapid administration may also produce an osmotic diuresis. These fluids are suitable for replacement of free water deficits (hypertonic dehydration) and for normal maintenance fluid requirements, provided potassium supplementation is given. A mixture of 2 Hartmann's : 1 glucose–saline with 20 mEq per litre of potassium can be combined for routine maintenance fluid replacement. Although 5% glucose is isotonic, the glucose uptake and metabolism following infusion means that it is essentially hypotonic.

Table 3 (overleaf) illustrates the composition of commonly used crystalloids.

Table 3   Composition of commonly used crystalloids

Fluid	Glucose (gram per litre)	Na (mmol per litre)	K (mmol per litre)	Cl (mmol per litre)	Ca (mmol per litre)	Buffer (mmol per litre)	Osmolarity (mosmol per litre)
Hartmann's	0	130	4	109	2	28	272
0.9% saline	0	154	0	154	0	0	308
Ringer's	0	148	4	156	2	0	310
0.18% NaCl + 4% glucose	40	31	0	31	0	0	260
5% glucose	50	0	0	0	0	0	252
7.2% NaCl	0	1232	0	1232	0	0	2464

The choice of fluid ultimately depends on the nature of the disease process and the composition of the fluid lost. As a general rule, losses should always be replaced with a fluid that is similar in composition to that which has been lost, but the vast majority of patients can be managed with a combination of a balanced (extracellular fluid-like) electrolyte solution, normal saline, and 5% glucose.

Hypertonic saline (7–7.5%) is a crystalloid but is markedly hypertonic to plasma. Given in small doses by slow i.v. injection it produces a haemodynamic effect similar to 60–90 ml per kg of crystalloid, largely by virtue of its osmotic effects, although increases in cardiac output and contractility are also claimed. It is extremely useful and cheap in larger patients and in combination with colloid appears to be the safest option for volume replacement in patients with head injury. The fluid should be avoided in patients with dehydration or hyperosmolar states.

Colloids

Colloids contain large molecules of varying compounds that remain within the circulating volume and exert a colloidal osmotic pressure, helping to maintain and expand circulating volume. The main reason for using colloids over crystalloids in volume resuscitation is their much longer retention in the intravascular space, resulting in a smaller required volume. The larger molecules maintain an osmotic gradient across the capillary wall that results in prolonged volume expansion. Plasma volume expansion may range from 70–170% of the infused amount. Colloids also have a role to play in hypoproteinaemic states associated with peripheral oedema or ascites. Gelatin-based colloids such as Haemaccel® and Gelofusin® have a much shorter duration of action than other colloids due to the large proportion of smaller molecules, and in some circumstances no significant advantage over hypertonic saline is offered. Starch-based colloids such as hetastarch and pentastarch have longer durations of action. There is also some evidence to suggest that starch-based colloids may be useful in reducing capillary permeability in conditions such as systemic inflammatory response syndrome (SIRS) and sepsis. Dextrans are glucose-based polymers used as colloids, but their use is not common due to effects on platelet function. Bleeding disorders have been detected in animals given large volumes of dextrans and starches. These complications appear to be uncommon in clinical practice. Risk of volume overload is greater with colloid administration, and patients with renal failure are particularly at risk due to reduced excretion of the compounds. The incidence of allergic reaction is generally low.

Potential indications for colloids include:

- certain situations where rapid infusion of large volumes of crystalloid would be contra-indicated
    - head injury
    - severe anaemia
    - ongoing or uncontrolled haemorrhage
- low plasma albumin, colloid osmotic pressure or peripheral oedema
- increased systemic vascular permeability.

Blood and blood products

In ideal circumstances, there can be little doubt that the most appropriate replacement fluid for acute severe blood loss is fresh, warmed, cross-matched whole blood. However, this is rarely the case and compromises often need to be made. Blood is commonly indicated if there is significant acute red cell loss (less well tolerated than chronic losses) likely to result in a PCV of less than 20%. This is difficult to assess in acute haemorrhage, as the PCV takes several hours to decline. Numerous equations are described to calculate volumes required; these do not take into account vascular responses and any transfusion should be titrated to the patient's response. Fresh whole blood or fresh plasma may also be given for coagulopathies and is often required in large volumes due to dilution.

More novel blood-related products include haemoglobin polymers such as Oxyglobin®, which is derived from bovine haemoglobin. No cross-matching is required and the shelf-life of the solution is long, although clinically apparent effects do not persist for as long as those of a blood transfusion. Oxyglobin® is a potent colloid and may also have some vascular effects; it should, therefore, be used with care in small patients and animals with cardiopulmonary disease. Due to the different oxygen-offloading mechanism, oxygen release to the tissues occurs more efficiently than with blood. The solution's low viscosity means that it may show better perfusion characteristics than whole blood.

Although the solution has obvious use as a blood substitute, its potential as an oxygen-carrying colloid is also interesting. Its volume expanding and flow properties may make it useful in situations where rapid restoration of tissue perfusion with oxygenated haemoglobin is required. A recent study in dogs with gastric dilation-volvulus showed that smaller volumes of oxyglobin were required to achieve volume resuscitation than were hetastarch, a colloid with similar oncotic properties. This might be due to the increased tissue oxygen delivery compared with hetastarch, or vasoconstrictive effects associated with oxyglobin use. Until clinical experience with the solution increases, its true role in fluid therapy and critical patient management remains to be defined, but in spite of its cost, the therapeutic potential of oxyglobin appears to be significant.

By what route can fluids be given?

Although the route of administration can depend on the type, duration and severity of the disorder, critically ill patients invariably require and receive fluids via a central or peripheral venous route. Advantages of the intravenous route include:

• maintenance of vascular access for drugs or emergencies

• rapid precise administration of large volumes of fluid

• central catheterisation permits measurement of central venous pressure (CVP).

Although the intravenous route is ubiquitous in critical care, it is not without complications. These can include:

• catheter infections and sepsis

• catheter thrombi

• cellulitis

• dislodgement and obstruction.

Any circulatory compromise should be managed by rapid intravascular administration via as wide and as short a catheter as possible (halving the radius of an i.v. catheter increases the resistance to flow along it by a factor of sixteen).

Other routes by which fluid therapy can be administered include subcutaneous, intraosseous and intraperitoneal routes.

Subcutaneous fluid therapy

Subcutaneous fluid therapy can be useful in more chronic cases where rapid administration of large volumes of fluid is not essential. This route can be painful and should only be used if the patient is receiving isotonic crystalloids.

Intraperitoneal fluid therapy

Intraperitoneal fluid can be administered in large volumes but the rate of absorption is not great. The risks of visceral penetration and peritonitis also exist.

Intraosseous fluid therapy

Intraosseous fluid administration relies on the presence of large venous networks in the diaphyses of long bones (humerus, tibia, femur), which can be accessed by introducing a needle into the diaphysis percutaneously. Bone marrow aspirate needles or spinal needles are suitable for this purpose. Following aseptic preparation of the site (usually proximal humerus or trochanteric fossa of the femur), local analgesic is infiltrated down to the level of the periosteum and the needle is passed through a stab incision. A combination of pressure and rotation locates the needle, after which, blood is aspirated to ensure correct placement.

Fluids can be given as fast intraosseously as they can intravenously, and this route is ideal in very small patients and those with venous collapse.

How much fluid and how fast?

Mild hypovolaemia can usually be corrected with rapid infusion of crystalloids at 20–30 ml per kg and carefully assessing the animal's response. In more severe cases, multiples of this volume can be administered up to one blood volume (90 ml per kg in dogs; 55–70 ml per kg in cats) or more in one hour. It is safest to administer rapid boluses of 15–20 ml per kg over 3–5 minutes rather than give large boluses.

Prior to administration of crystalloids at this rate, the following points should be addressed.

1 Is there evidence of heart disease causing cardiogenic shock? Usually cardiogenic shock is suspected if auscultation of the heart reveals a murmur or arrhythmia, and the animal is in respiratory distress. If any of these findings are present, fluid therapy must be initially cautious.

2 Does this patient have any history or signs of dyspnoea or respiratory disease? The presence of lung disease can increase the risk of fluid therapy and a cautious approach with regard to fluid volumes and rates should be used.

3 Could this animal have pale mucous membranes due to anaemia rather than decreased blood volume? This question can usually be easily answered by PCV measurement as part of the database that should always be obtained before starting fluid therapy in emergency patients. If severe anaemia is present, a whole blood or packed red cell transfusion should be considered immediately.

4 Does the patient have any indication of head trauma or intracranial disease? Over-administration of any fluid type in a patient with cerebral contusions or ongoing bleeding may aggravate increases in intracranial pressure.

5 Is there evidence of uncontrolled haemorrhage? Numerous studies have shown that aggressive fluid administration in the face of uncontrolled bleeding increases mortality, probably by dilution of platelets and clotting factors, reduced viscosity and clot disruption. Every effort should be made to control bleeding (including counter-pressure bandaging in the case of intra-abdominal bleeding); fluids should be administered at rates sufficient to maintain acceptable perfusion rather than aggressive restoration of volume.

Patients with dehydration in the absence of poor perfusion can be administered fluids at lower rates. An estimated deficit based on historical losses can be arrived at and combined with the patient's maintenance fluid requirement (about 2 ml per kg per hour) to give an infusion rate. In most cases, a rate of 2–3 times maintenance is sufficient for correction of dehydration over a 24-hour period, providing that ongoing losses do not increase and patient monitoring is adequate.

When should fluid therapy be stopped?

Cessation of intravenous fluids occurs when the patient's perfusion is normalised, urine output is normalised, and normal maintenance fluid and electrolyte requirements are able to be met by voluntary food and fluid intake. Knowing when this point has been reached depends on careful monitoring of the patient.

What should be monitored?

Many parameters are generally considered to be of import in monitoring hypovolaemia and dehydration. These generally fall into three main categories: assessments derived from basic physical examination, laboratory-based measurements, and objectively measured or calculated variables. These parameters can be subdivided as follows:

- assessments derived from basic physical examination
    - heart rate and rhythm
    - pulse rate and profile
    - mucous membrane colour and moisture
    - capillary refill time and vigour
    - skin turgor
    - mentation
    - core : periphery temperature gradient
- laboratory-based measurements
    - lactate
    - PCV or TPP
    - acid–base status
- objectively measured or calculated variables
    - urine output
    - CVP
    - arterial blood pressure.

Assessments derived from basic physical examination

Regularly repeated basic physical assessment still forms the cornerstone of patient monitoring. Heart rate and pulse rate should normalise (80–120 bpm in dogs; 160–180 bpm in cats) rapidly in response to fluid administration in patients with simple hypovolaemia. A persistent tachycardia should prompt an aggressive search for sites of fluid loss or haemorrhage; in addition to this, the possibility of pain-associated tachycardia and the patient's analgesic requirements should be re-assessed. Both the strength and duration of the palpable pulse wave should increase, and the peripheral pulses should become easily palpable. Mucous membranes should resume much of their pink coloration (cats generally have paler mucous membranes than dogs) and capillary refill time (CRT) should return to the normal value of 1–1.5 seconds (shorter than normal CRT in septic patients should not be misinterpreted). A rapid return to normal levels of alertness and the presence of warm, pink digits should also be expected (patients with greater than a 10 °F difference between deep rectal and toe-web temperatures are likely to have inadequate peripheral perfusion). In patients with uncomplicated hypovolaemia (due to arrested haemorrhage, effusions, isotonic dehydration) the majority of these parameters should normalise within 30–60 minutes of initiating fluid therapy.

Laboratory-based measurements

Measurement of plasma lactate is now well-established not only as a means of determining the severity of tissue hypoperfusion, but also as a means of monitoring and guiding therapy. The reference range for plasma lactate concentration in normal dogs is less than 2.5 mmol per litre. Values in excess of 10 mmol per litre represent severe hypovolaemia.

Measurement of PCV and TPP is important to ensure that excessive haemodilution does not occur; a PCV above 25% and TPP above 45% are desirable endpoints.

Although the presence of co-existing disorders may confound interpretation, the majority of hypovolaemic patients develop a degree of metabolic acidosis (usually accompanied by a high anion gap). A gradual improvement in plasma pH and decrease in the calculated base deficit (i.e. a less negative value) are, therefore, reasonably reliable indicators of improved perfusion.

Objectively measured or calculated variables

Urine production correlates reasonably well with renal blood flow and cardiac output. Urine production of 0.5–1.5 ml per kg per hour with specific gravity within the normal range is generally considered to be acceptable in both cats and dogs. Failure of adequate urine production should invoke further assessment of the patient's cardiovascular status, checking of indwelling urinary catheters for obstruction, leakage, improper placement or inadvertent removal, or the possibility of renal shutdown.

Arterial blood pressure monitoring is not a sensitive test for hypovolaemia, as animals with intact compensatory mechanisms typically maintain relatively normal arterial pressures until they are near death. However, arterial hypotension in animals with uncomplicated hypovolaemia is a major source of concern demanding an immediate and aggressive therapeutic response. Animals with disrupted compensatory responses (such as might be due to septic shock, severe trauma, or anaesthetic drugs) may develop life-threatening hypotension at less severe levels of hypovolaemia, and arterial pressure monitoring in those patients should be routinely considered. Direct monitoring of arterial pressure is infinitely superior to non-invasive methods, and has maintained accuracy at lower pressures.

Accurate measurement of CVP provides invaluable information about circulating volume status relative to cardiac performance. The CVP is the pressure within the intrathoracic portions of the cranial or caudal vena cava (Figure 7, overleaf).

CVP is measured clinically for two reasons:

• to gain information about cardiac function
• to gain information about blood volume relative to vascular capacity.

The central venous catheter should ideally be positioned with the tip positioned in the cranial vena cava just cranial to the right atrium (when introduced into the external jugular vein) or in the caudal vena cava just caudal to the right atrium (when introduced into a pelvic limb vein). A clinically acceptable substitute in cats is to position the tip within the abdominal caudal vena cava.

Electronic CVP monitoring is preferred whenever possible because of its speed and accuracy. When using a water column manometer, substantial inaccuracies in CVP measurements (up to 20 cmH₂O over- or under-estimation) are possible in different patient body positions. These are easily avoided by electronic measurement.

The numerical CVP may be routinely interpreted as the electronically determined mean pressure value.

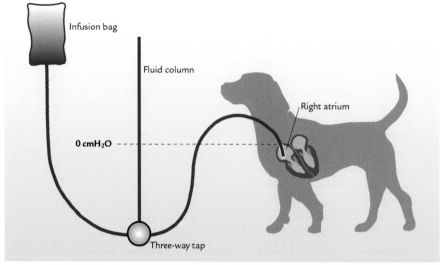

Figure 7   Central venous pressure

Using CVP to guide fluid administration

Ensure the patient is in the same position for each measurement.

Normal CVP = 5–10 cmH$_2$O

Rapid infusion (less than 3 minutes) of 15 ml per kg of crystalloid or 5 ml per kg of colloid into a normovolaemic animal with normal cardiac function results in a mild increase in CVP (2–4 cmH$_2$0) that returns to baseline within 15 minutes.

A minimal increase or no increase in CVP implies that the vascular volume is markedly reduced relative to cardiac performance.

If the CVP rises and returns to baseline rapidly (less than 5 minutes), this implies that there is reduced vascular volume and that the initial volume load has been easily accommodated.

The fluid boluses are repeated and CVP response is monitored until the CVP rises with the challenge and takes progressively longer to return towards the baseline value.

A large initial increase in CVP (more than 4 cmH$_2$O) implies reduced cardiac compliance or increased venous blood volume or both.

A slow (15 minutes) return towards baseline indicates that blood volume is close to normal.

References

DiBartola S P (2001), 'Introduction to fluid therapy'. In *Fluid Therapy in Small Animal Practice* (2nd edn), ed. S P DiBartola, pp. 265–80. New York: W B Saunders Ltd

5 Cardiopulmonary arrest and cardiopulmonary-cerebral resuscitation

Cardiopulmonary arrest (CPA) represents the ultimate emergency, and all nursing staff within a veterinary clinic or hospital should not only be able to recognise when a CPA has occurred, but should also be able to assist in performing basic cardiopulmonary life support, as they are often the first individuals to detect that an arrest has occurred. As nursing staff are usually involved in stocking and maintenance of emergency 'crash' boxes and trolleys and assisting clinicians in resuscitative protocols, a thorough working knowledge of the principles and procedures involved in more advanced resuscitation techniques is also highly desirable.

Respiratory arrest – sudden or gradual cessation of respiratory activity that will lead to cardiorespiratory arrest unless rapid measures to establish a patent airway and effective artificial ventilation are established.

Cardiorespiratory or cardiopulmonary arrest – sudden or gradual cessation of respiratory and effective cardiac activity.

Basic life support – establishing a patent airway, performing positive pressure ventilation, and generating a circulation by performing chest compressions.

Advanced life support – basic life support plus medical interventions intended to optimise chances of recovery. These include:

- resuscitative drugs

- electrical defibrillation

- post-resuscitation life support.

Causes of cardiopulmonary arrest

Along with duration of CPA, the underlying cause is probably the most significant factor affecting the patient's chances of survival from an arrest. Causes of CPA can be broadly classified as follows:

- severe cardiovascular disease or trauma
- severe hypovolaemia or hypoperfusion
- hyperthermia
- hypothermia
- acid–base disturbances (principally acidosis)
- electrolyte disturbances

- hypoglycaemia
- toxins causing cardiopulmonary depression
- sedative or anaesthetic drug overdose
- hypoxia
- hypercapnia (excessive retention or build-up of carbon dioxide)
- severe anaemia
- head trauma or intracranial disease.

Relative or absolute anaesthetic or sedative drug overdose still remains a common cause of CPA in dogs and cats. Major respiratory distress and subsequent respiratory arrest due to obstructive airway disease or pleural cavity disease (pneumothorax, diaphragmatic rupture, pleural fluid) is also a frequent precursor to full cardiopulmonary arrest in critically ill or injured patients. Many of the causes listed above are potentially treatable and curable if detected early; CPA is always a far easier condition to prevent than it is to treat.

Be prepared

Adequate preparation is essential to reduce the time lag between recognition of the arrest and the start of resuscitative efforts. A highly mobile trolley or case containing all essential equipment for resuscitation should be available, and all staff should know of its whereabouts at all times. In larger facilities, more than one such case should be easily accessible; some duplication of essential equipment may therefore be necessary.

Items to be stocked in a resuscitation trolley should consist of the following:

- for the airway
    - wide range of endotracheal tube sizes (3–14 mm), pre-tied and with syringes attached to cuffs
    - flexible stylets or tube guidewires
    - lubricant
    - mouth gag
    - laryngoscope + wide range of blades (alternative light sources are acceptable)
    - preconnected 2 ml syringe barrel + 7 mm ET tube + Oxford connector + 14G 2" needle (for trans-tracheal oxygen delivery)
    - cricothyroidotomy or tracheotomy kit (if available)
- for breathing
    - oxygen source, anaesthetic breathing system
    - resuscitator or Ambu device
- for circulation
    - equipment for i.v. access (cannulae, tape, T-ports, stopcocks etc.)
    - intraosseous needle
    - small surgical cutdown pack with scalpel blades + handle, curved Mayo scissors, retractors

- intravenous fluids + fluid administration sets
- materials for abdominal counter-pressure bandaging
- portable ECG monitor (if available)
- drugs for emergency use
    - atropine (pre-drawn)
    - adrenaline (pre-drawn)
    - lignocaine (pre-drawn)
    - sodium bicarbonate
    - calcium chloride.

A stock list should be kept with each box or trolley, which should be checked and restocked weekly and immediately after each resuscitation episode.

The number of suitably trained and experienced personnel is also critical to the success of any resuscitation attempt. Cardiopulmonary–cerebral resuscitation (CPCR) is effectively impossible to perform alone and is very difficult with two operators. The presence of a third person to perform ventilations while the first two perform chest compressions and administer drugs and fluids is more efficient.

Recognising an arrest

Early recognition of impending or actual respiratory or cardiorespiratory arrest is essential if fatality is to be avoided, and all nursing staff should be aware of the signs associated with these events. Common signs of imminent respiratory arrest include the following:

- persistent mouth-breathing (cats)
- respiratory distress in lateral recumbency (cats, often with dilated pupils)
- sudden development of limb rigidity and opisthotonus
- sudden slowing of respiratory rate
- bizarre, exaggerated or irregular chest wall movements
- obvious cyanosis.

Other signs indicating development of cardiopulmonary arrest include:

- extreme pallor of mucous membranes
- absence of a palpable central pulse
- absence of respiratory movement
- eye central within orbit
- bilaterally dilated unresponsive pupils
- absent corneal reflex
- lack of bleeding at site of surgery or trauma
- very dark blood at site of surgery or trauma
- involuntary urination or defecation.

Treating an arrest

When initially assessing the suspected arrest patient, oxygen should first be administered by mask or direct flow and assistance should be called for. Primary survey should address the three fundamental questions.

Primary survey

Airway – Does the patient have a patent airway?

Breathing – Is the patient making regular coordinated efforts to breathe?

Circulation – Does the patient have a palpable or audible heartbeat and palpable pulses?

Do not assume that an animal has a patent airway if it is already anaesthetised and intubated – always check tube patency. Recognition of a palpable pulse may be difficult if a patient is severely bradycardic, as is often the case with respiratory arrest. Careful palpation is essential. If there is any doubt as to whether an arrest has occurred, it is safer to assume that it has and treat accordingly, rather than waste valuable time trying to detect a pulse (patients with very weak or slow pulses will invariably need some form of acute support).

Airway

Rapid and secure airway access is essential in the management of respiratory arrest and cardiopulmonary arrest precipitated by respiratory disease or depression. The easiest approach may be to position the animal in sternal recumbency and extend the head and neck; this will straighten the airway. Intubation is a valuable skill and should be practised with the patient in lateral and dorsal recumbency as well. The mouth should be held open and the tongue drawn forward to optimise the view of the larynx; a dry swab may be needed to help grip the tongue if excessive saliva or vomitus is present. A laryngoscope or suitable light source should be directed at the larynx and rapid visual inspection should be performed. A suitable endotracheal tube should then be placed, the cuff inflated and the tube secured in place. Compressing the chest to check tube placement can sometimes be misleading, as gastric compression may occur and give a false impression of correct placement. Visualisation or digital palpation of the tube passing through the larynx are usually more reliable methods.

If an endotracheal tube is not immediately available, mouth-to-nose expired air ventilation can be performed. External chest compressions alone will generate some air movement within the respiratory tract; this process can be augmented by giving mask oxygen simultaneously.

Conscious patients with imminent respiratory arrest will obviously not tolerate intubation without sedation or anaesthesia, although this is invariably preferable to waiting for a full respiratory arrest and loss of consciousness to occur before intubating the patient. Nursing staff should, therefore, ensure that adequate drugs and equipment for rapid intravenous induction of anaesthesia are to hand. These animals are often exquisitely sensitive to the cardiodepressant effects of such agents, and the clinician should administer induction agents slowly and to effect rather than using predetermined doses based on bodyweight. Alternatively, low doses of potent, rapidly acting opioids or benzodiazepines either alone or in combination may be adequate.

Breathing

Once a patent airway has been secured, three to five rapid 'rescue' breaths should be administered. In many patients with simple respiratory arrest, this may be enough to provide sufficient oxygenation and allow recovery. It is important not to hyperventilate or use excessive airway pressures; a normal degree of chest wall movement should be produced. If airway pressure is being measured, it should not exceed 20 cmH$_2$O (in order to avoid lung damage). Some conditions may, however, need higher pressures to achieve effective ventilation. If there is a high degree of resistance to lung inflation, the cause should be investigated aggressively, starting with a re-assessment of the airway.

Ventilation rates of 10–15 breaths per minute are usually adequate. Use of 100% oxygen is ideal, but ventilation should not be delayed if it is not immediately available, as room air contains 21% oxygen (expired air contains 16% oxygen) and is sufficient to sustain life in the intervening period. Manual resuscitators automatically refill with room air if the bag is released after compression.

Circulation

Chest compression is the universally accepted method of generating a circulation. This is thought to work by two mechanisms.

1 The cardiac pump, in which compression of the chest results in cardiac compression and squeezes blood out of the heart in the normal direction. This is probably the most important mechanism in cats and small dogs, and in the early stages of an arrest when the heart muscle is still compliant.

2 The thoracic pump, in which compression of the chest causes an increase in pressure within the thorax, resulting in intermittent compression of the great vessels returning blood to the heart. Thicker-walled arteries stay patent, resulting in forward flow of blood. This is probably more important in larger dogs and later on in the arrest, when the heart muscle 'stiffens'.

Compression is performed in a number of different ways depending on the patient's size and shape.

1 In cats and small dogs, compression is most easily performed by cupping a hand around the sternum and compressing the thorax directly over the heart between thumb and fingers. This also allows any returning heartbeat to be palpated.

2 In larger, deep-chested dogs, compression is performed over the highest area of the chest with the animal in right lateral recumbency.

3 In round or barrel-chested breeds, chest compressions are effective with the dog in dorsal recumbency. Compression is centred in the midline over the caudal aspect of the sternum. Although effective, this may be more difficult to perform.

Compression should be performed at a rate of at least 100 compressions per minute in order to be effective, with compression and relaxation phases being of equal duration. The strength of compression may need to be varied until a femoral or (preferably) sublingual pulse can be palpated. A Doppler blood flow probe can be inserted under the upper eyelid to detect flow in the central retinal artery if available.

Alternating chest and abdominal compressions have been shown to improve results in some studies of CPCR; however, this can be difficult to achieve and may result in damage to abdominal organs. Sustained compression of the hindlimbs and abdomen can help optimise blood volume; this can be performed with counter-pressure bandaging.

Internal cardiac compression

Performing an emergency thoracotomy to allow direct compression of the heart is obviously a major procedure, but direct cardiac compression achieves better cardiac output and more effective flow to the cerebral and coronary circulations than indirect compression. Indications for immediate open-chest resuscitation are as follows:

- severe pleural cavity disease (pneumothorax, pleural fluid, ruptured diaphragm)
- pericardial effusion and cardiac tamponnade
- penetrating chest wall wounds
- major chest wall injuries.

Other situations where open-chest cardiopulmonary resuscitation can be seriously considered:

- haemoperitoneum
- arrests in dogs over 20 kg
- unwitnessed arrests
- if closed-chest CPCR is not effective within 2–5 minutes.

A rapid (surgical preparation is unnecessary) left lateral incision is performed at the 6th intercostal space. Ventilation should be halted as the pleura is incised to allow the lungs to fall away from the chest wall. The pericardium is opened at the cardiac apex and the heart is gently grasped and compressed from apex to base. Compression rates are similar to those for closed-chest CPCR.

Defibrillation

Defibrillation requires an electrocardiographic diagnosis before it can be treated. The three main arrhythmias associated with cardiac arrest are:

- asystole – absence of any electrical activity
- electrical–mechanical dissociation (sometimes known as pulseless electrical activity) – the ECG rhythm may appear surprisingly normal, but no mechanical cardiac activity is present
- ventricular fibrillation – bizarre, chaotic waveform.

Electrical defibrillation is a vital component of advanced cardiac life support, as there are no other consistently reliable methods for treating ventricular fibrillation. Ventricular fibrillation is a far more common arrest rhythm in humans than in veterinary patients, and is the only rhythm that can be treated with any regular success. If ventricular fibrillation is evident on the ECG, then the clinician should administer three external shocks of 2–4 joules per kg in rapid succession. An electrical defibrillator effectively stores a huge amount of current which is discharged rapidly, allowing a more normal rhythm to establish. Defibrillation should only be performed by a suitably experienced clinician, and no other personnel should be in physical contact with the patient or the table on which it is lying during defibrillation, as severe shock, burns or even death could result. Good electrical contact between the defibrillator paddles and the patient is achieved with generous amount of electrode gel (do not use surgical spirit as this will ignite). A burning smell after discharge suggests poor contact.

Drugs

As yet, there are no conclusive clinically based studies in human or veterinary patients to show that use of resuscitative drugs during CPCR increases survival. It is, therefore, important to ensure that the basic life support measures (airway, breathing, circulation) are performed early and performed well, as this probably has the greatest impact on survival.

Routes of drug administration in CPCR are important. The following options exist:

- peripheral vein – external cardiac massage must be effective for this route to be useful; injection may be followed by fluid bolus to help access to the central circulation
- central vein – route of choice if available (a cutdown may be required); allows rapid delivery of the drug to the site of action
- intraosseous – a useful route in CPCR as the vascular network within the bone remains patent
- intratracheal – rapid absorption occurs across the mucosal membrane; the drug should be doubled and should be mixed in 2–3 ml of saline, delivery should be followed by two breaths
- intracardiac – contra-indicated unless the heart is directly visible; blind injection may damage coronary vessels and nerves, and intramyocardial injection may cause arrhythmias.

Although many different drugs have been used in CPCR, the principal agents used are relatively few. They are briefly discussed below.

Adrenaline (epinephrine)

Adrenaline improves coronary and cerebral blood flow and may make ventricular fibrillation easier to defibrillate. It is usually used at doses of 0.1–0.2 mg per kg.

Atropine

Atropine is useful in the management of vagally mediated or drug-induced severe bradycardias or bradyarrhythmias. Its use in asystole may not be effective, but it is unlikely to do any harm. The usual dose is 0.02–0.04 mg per kg.

Lignocaine

Although not a true resuscitation drug, lignocaine is invaluable in the management of ventricular arrhythmias and tachycardias (bolus dose 2–8 mg per kg) and for use by infusion (25–75 μg per kg per minute) to control post-resuscitation arrhythmias.

Sodium bicarbonate

Once a popular drug, sodium bicarbonate is now confined to treatment of confirmed metabolic acidosis, hyperkalaemia (raised blood potassium level), barbiturate overdoses (though not on a resuscitative basis) or in prolonged arrests where acidosis is suspected. As the drug inactivates pulmonary surfactant, it should not be given intratracheally. Doses of 1–2 mmol per kg should be given very slowly.

Calcium chloride

Calcium chloride is only indicated for pre-existing hyperkalaemia or hypocalcaemia, or if overdose of calcium-channel blocking drugs occurs. Do not mix with bicarbonate-containing solutions. Doses of 0.5–1 ml per kg of a 10% solution are usually used.

Signs of effective resuscitation

Return of spontaneous circulation is usually the first noted change. If resuscitative attempts are proving successful, palpable pulses may return and mucous membrane coloration may improve. Pupils may become responsive to light and the eyes may shift position within the orbit, although these changes may not occur for some time. Spontaneous breathing may return rapidly if the arrest was respiratory or very short in duration; otherwise it may take many hours to return. Consciousness is not immediate, but an increase in awareness may occur, necessitating a light plane of general anaesthesia to allow chest closure if open-chest CPR was performed.

The decision to stop CPCR is made by the clinician in consultation with all those involved in the resuscitation attempt. CPCR is significantly less likely to be successful in an animal with major pre-existing disease and is probably inappropriate in some patients; this should be discussed with the owner before any decisions are made, as some owners will not want CPCR to be performed and may strongly object to open-chest resuscitation. Resuscitative attempts lasting beyond 20–25 minutes without any obvious signs of return of spontaneous circulation are extremely unlikely to be successful.

Post-resuscitation care and life support

Management of the successfully resuscitated patient, especially after prolonged arrest is an enormous nursing commitment and an in-depth discussions is beyond the scope of this book. However, the aims of patient care and monitoring after the return of spontaneous circulation, can be summarised as follows.

1 Maintenance of normal ventilation (elimination of carbon dioxide) and oxygenation, for which the patient must have a clear airway. If the patient is still unconscious, the endotracheal tube should remain in place. All post-arrest patients should be maintained on supplemental oxygen. If less than 100% oxygen is required, the patient may be able to be maintained on nasal oxygen. If the patient is still intubated but breathing spontaneously, then an oxygen cannula can be inserted down the endotracheal tube. If the patient is unable to ventilate adequately (based on blood gases, capnometry), positive pressure ventilation must be maintained. This is frequently indicated in the immediate post-arrest period.

2 Maintenance of normal circulating volume, arterial and central venous pressures ideally requires invasive pressure monitoring, and drugs such as dobutamine may be needed to maintain adequate pressure. Fluid input should be monitored together with urine output, and patients should be carefully monitored for signs of fluid overload.